ARTHUR A. OAKMAN
Themes from His Radio Sermons

ARTHUR A. OAKMAN
Themes from His Radio Sermons

Edited by Stephen Gregson

Herald Publishing House, Independence, Missouri
1978

COPYRIGHT © 1978
Herald Publishing House

Library of Congress Cataloging in Publication Data

Oakman, Arthur A.
  Arthur A. Oakman: radio sermons.

  1. Reorganized Church of Jesus Christ of Latter Day Saints
—Sermons. 2. Sermons, American. I. Gregson, Stephen.
BX8676.029A77   252'.09'33   78-7712
ISBN 0-8309-0216-3

Printed in the United States of America

CONTENTS

PREFACE

He is remembered by many for his resonant tones that traveled the airwaves as he expressed his deep desire to bring people to Christ and shared his enlightenment as to the workings of the Holy Spirit. Arthur Oakman often introduced his radio sermons by a poem or short quotation. Here is one by William Temple which he used:

"He who so loved is not self-occupied or concerned with doctrines of his own person. But he spontaneously and with conscious appropriateness does what only God can do. He is not self-analytical but he is self-revealing: and the self that he reveals is more than human, more than superhuman, it is specifically divine.

"He is the Lord of life and death: he is the guide of all human history. And nothing can be done but under his supremacy."

THEOLOGY

After hearing a sermon on the Incarnation, an army officer approached and said, "I enjoyed your sermon. It sounded fine. But I have no use for all that theory stuff. Of course, I know there's a God. I have felt him many times. I know he exists. That's why I do not go for all these theories and formulas you preachers talk about. When you have known the real thing as I have, all your creeds seem unreal and unnecessary."

This language reminds one of a verse in the last poem of Emily Brontë:

Vain are the thousand creeds
That move men's hearts,
unutterably vain,
Worthless as withered weeds,
Or idle froth amid the boundless main,

This attitude is very prevalent. A great many people feel that when they turn from a contemplation of the divine glory in nature to a study of the creeds or of theology, they are turning from something real, warm, and vital to something artificial, cold, and dead. Practical men—men who are dealing with everyday problems—have a tendency to think that theology is unrelated to their affairs.

Three hundred years ago John Donne, dean of St. Paul's, asked the question: "Why doe the young menne so much study theologie?" Such a question would never be thought of today. The study of theology, the appreciation of God, his existence and relation to the universe, does not trouble young men now. And this is a great pity, for our generation is losing touch, by ignorant default, with the one great source of spiritual and moral power available to it.

The ordinary man, we are told, "wants plain, practical religion, not theology." But if he is not a fool, the plain man wants the most accurate ideas possible about God and wants them clearly and simply expressed. This means that the plain man *does* want theology. Theology is the science of God and of the relation between God and nature.

This is a scientific age. Indeed, science is its chief glory. So it is quite irrational to be unconcerned about science in the moral and spiritual realm while accepting the ministrations of those high priests, the scientists, who part the veil and step into the hidden mysteries of the temporal world and bring back practical knowledge which ministers to our bodily comfort. Of course theology is important. Once it was known as "the queen of the sciences." And it was known thus not because it included the detailed knowledge of all the other sciences but because it sought to show their underlying principle and demonstrated how they were related to the knowledge of God.

When the army officer turned from a contemplation of the sense of divine presence to listen to a theological dissertation, he was turning from something very real to something less real. Christian experience is always prior to and more fundamental than the creeds. When a man looks at the ocean from the beach, and then goes and looks at a map, he is turning from a contemplation of waves and sand and sunshine to a bit of colored paper—from something very real to that which is less real. But the map has behind it a massive experience built up by thousands of people who have sailed the seas and charted the oceans. It is a diagrammatic representation of a historical experience. Its function is to represent that experience and aid those who desire to go across the ocean to other lands. As long as we stand on the beach and are content with our own glimpses of the Eternal, we do not need theology. But if we want to go to the promised land, if the experience of those who have found the promised land is to be our experience also, then we must use the map—we must study theology.

A walk on the beach may be a beautiful and uplifting experience, but it brings us up against an insurmountable barrier, a *mysterium tremendum* across which we cannot go without the aid of those who have ventured before and have left in the record of their experience—in theology—a chart, a compass, and a craft upon which we may safely sail. The trouble with the army officer was that his experience led him nowhere. And that's the trouble with much of our modern life—it is going nowhere. It has no effective leadership.

Of course, studying the map will, of itself, lead nowhere either. Merely learning the Christian doctrines, even gaining the ability to describe and explain them, is less thrilling than walking on the beach or listening to music or smelling flowers. Doctrines and creeds aren't God; they are only a kind of description of how we may find him. Like the map, they point the way and are valuable only to those who *want to go somewhere.* But smelling the flowers and listening to the music is not eternal life either. Feeling God in nature is no substitute for receiving his Spirit in our lives, and thus receiving his life in ours. It may be all thrills and very enjoyable. But to sail our frail bark across "the void of mystery and dread" which looms ahead, we must "take knowledge" of those who have gone before, the greatest of whom is Christ Jesus our Lord. Theology is thus the primary practical study for those who want to make something of their lives—for those who want to "get somewhere" worthwhile.

Many years ago when books were scarce and education was limited, the average man could get along with a few simple ideas about God and the human soul. But now nearly everyone is literate, reads, hears, talks, and discusses. The consequence is not that people have no ideas about God, but that they have all sorts of wrong, hazy, out-of-date ideas. All sorts of notions are prevalent now and are sponsored as novelties, new discoveries, new theories. But these notions were discussed and disposed of centuries ago by competent theologians and by saints. For instance, the idea prevails abroad that Christ was a great moral teacher, and if only we would take his advice we could build a new social order and end all wars. "The Golden Rule" is supposed to be the essence of Christ's teachings, and of course "everyone ought to follow it"... but nobody does. Such hazy thinking tells precisely nothing about Christianity and is of no practical importance at all.

If Christianity is just another piece of good moral advice, it isn't worth bothering about. The world is full of good advice. Plato, Aristotle, and Confucius gave sound moral advice, years before Jesus came, and the world has not listened to them. Why would it listen to Jesus?

● ● ●

Just as soon as one begins to study theology he finds that Christianity bears no resemblance to the popular ideas about morality and Christ's being a moral teacher. He discovers that Christ is reported to be the Son of God. The Scriptures affirm that those who believe on him also have power given them to be the sons of God. They say also that Christ came here to die for us and that somehow his death has the power to save us from death.

These utterances are difficult to comprehend, but why would they be simple or easy when Christianity claims to be telling about another world or sphere of existence behind and beyond this one? Surely the study of any science is not easy, so why should one expect the study of the science of the knowledge of God to be easier than, say, anthropology? So even if Christianity is not easy, its claim to be a new way of life, if true, is certainly worth all the effort we can expend to obtain knowledge of it.

We may or may not be, as Henley affirms, the "captain of our souls." No sensible captain ever put out to sea with inadequate charts and maps, faulty instruments, no safeguards against storm and wind, and no means to get to his destination. Wise people study, as best they can, the experiences through which others have passed in their search for adequate ideas about God, because in this spiritual heritage they find ample means to sail the sea of life safely. The Scriptures advise all to study theology: "Be always ready to give a reason for the hope that is within you."

Theology is the science of God and of his relation to the universe. Science is a word with which all of us are familiar. We feel that we are on safe ground if what we do or have or think is "scientific." The various sciences—anthropology, geology, zoology, physics—are simply departments of man's experience of the universe which have been segregated or "isolated" from the rest for any purposes of study. His experience may be, indeed must be, enlarged and expanded through the use of various instruments— telescope, microscope, and many others. Thus the heavens seem nearer and the earth enlarged by means of these instruments. But the subject matter of the sciences is always the universe or some portion of it. The universe is an expression of creative will—exhibiting the purpose of God—and is sustained in being by his matchless power.

Theology seeks to go behind creation to the Creator. It endeavors to gain knowledge of the "friend behind phenomena." Of course, as a man's character is seen to some extent in his work, so also is the divine character disclosed to some extent in the universe—God's handiwork—but only "to some extent." Science is related to theology as the knowledge of a man's work is related to knowledge of the man. But no man is completely revealed in his work alone. Certain characteristics only are displayed there because a full and complete knowledge or understanding can be obtained only through personal communion with the man himself.

So, then, theology takes account of the testimony of those who have held communion with God, as well as observing how God's character is shown forth in creation. The study of God at work in nature is known as "natural religion." That which deals with the revelation of him in the testimony of those who have had communion with him is called "revealed religion." Theology includes both of these and seeks to bring them into complete harmony.

All sciences rest, in the last analysis, on faith: faith in the rationality of the universe, faith in the trustworthiness of human reason to correspond with the rational universe, faith in the testimony of fellow scientists, faith in the existence of such things as time and space, mind and matter, cause and effect. Science has doctrines also. Some of these are the uniformity of law, the impartiality of phenomena, the possibility of framing statements of these laws. Science is an expression of faith, and knowledge is the fruit of scientific research which is, in turn, an adjustment to the assumptions of such faith.

Scientists themselves recognize this fact. Sir William Hamilton affirms, "Faith—belief—is the organ by

which we apprehend that which is beyond knowledge."
Faith is never opposed to *reason*, but it is sometimes antithetical to *sight*. The greatest single spiritual factor in scientific research is faith. So also in theology, faith is the basic spiritual requirement in the search for knowledge of God. Faith is neither opinion nor imagination. It is the "invincible surmise," the certitude within the soul which is based upon the very nature of our existence as rational creatures.

All scientists evince a love for truth. This love of truth gives the reason power to apprehend the truth. All art rests upon a love of beauty which gives the artist power to recognize beauty. So the power to apprehend moral righteousness is also inseparable from a love for the right. The power to recognize and commune with God is also supremely inseparable from a love for God. And the love for God can be induced only as that love is made manifest and he himself made desirable to man.

The mathematics of sound or the mechanics of harmony can, by themselves, give no actual appreciation for music. They can enhance an appreciation already possessed by the listener, but music is apprehended by musical sense—"an ear for music." Those who are tone deaf may expound a doctrine of musical mathematics perfectly, but they will never come to the heart of the matter. The science of optics may be rationally apprehended by a blind man, but he will not thereby be enabled to see. Logic and science can give us no knowledge of the beauty of a sunset or the glory of a righteous life. Love for the beautiful and the right precedes knowledge of the beautiful and right.

This is further illustrated as we remember that the word *wisdom* comes from a Greek word *sapentia* or *sapere* which means "to taste." The intellect alone is not qualified to know God; the heart must be disposed toward him first. So the scripture is quite scientific when it advises men to "taste and see how gracious the Lord is, blessed is the man that trusts in him." *Taste* precedes *sight*. Wisdom is more than intellect. Experience with God conditions knowledge of him.

The organ through which we come to know God is our whole selves—the heart and soul of us, the whole disposition. An astronomer who always used a dirty lens on his telescope would gain a very partial and even incorrect knowledge of his science. Pure white sunlight can never be fully reflected from a dirty mirror. While scientists use instruments external to themselves to gain knowledge of the universe, the instrument through which men come to know God is not external—it is the whole self. If the self is unclean and impure (and all selves who ever lived except one were and are to some extent impure), then the knowledge of God will be partial and even faulty. A wicked nation or a filthy mind will apprehend a grotesque idea of God which will confirm those who hold it in their wickedness and filth.

The testimony of theology is that once in one person, Jesus Christ, the mirror of the human soul was wholly clean and without blemish, and therefore in him and from him alone we have reflected completely the knowledge of God.

So theology is a science, and indeed the most important science there is. Of course it is not easy. It is only the false and ready-made man-made religions and ideas that are easy. Facts are never easy; they are stubborn and unyielding. Jesus Christ, it is said, is the "Son of Fact."

● ● ●

Science, commonly so-called, is at root a spiritual enterprise dealing with physical facts—with the world as seen, with the temporal order. Theology is also a spiritual enterprise, but it *interprets* the temporal and visible world in terms of spiritual facts.

In each endeavor the underlying motivating factors are identical. Faith undergirds all human activity, but the area in which these spiritual factors are employed is different in each case. Science deals with the temporal order. Theology includes as one area of activity—and only as one area of activity— the temporal order and goes beyond to the spiritual unseen world which is behind and beyond the temporal. But the whole universe—seen and unseen— is one; and because it is one and not many, science and theology are intimately related and truth agrees with itself everywhere and always.

The distinction between natural and revealed religion has been pointed out. More must be said about this, and more must be said about science and Christianity. Basically the distinction is this: Such thought and doctrine about God as could be conducted without reference to church, Bible, or revelation is known as natural religion; such thought and doctrine as is built on the authority of the Bible and the church is revealed religion. So the distinction prevailed widely many years ago and led men to think that there was antagonism between reason and revelation.

The breach is not now so wide. The inspired utterances of the nineteenth century prophet have aided many people to bridge this gap; and Section 85 of the Doctrine and Covenants remains the pivotal statement which joins natural and revealed religion, science and philosophy, with religion. Some have confidently asserted, "Science does not deny God; she does better; she makes him unnecessary." Not many believe now that science has made God unnecessary, but strong tension still prevails in many minds between the canons and methods of science and the basic doctrines of the Christian religion.

For example, as recently as 1928 Dr. Elmer Barnes stated before the American Association for the Advancement of Science that discoveries in astrophysics had made it impossible for intelligent men aware of the advancement of science to believe any longer in the conception of God known as Christian. He went on to say that God, if he exists at all, must be the God of the whole universe. The Christian idea was framed when men thought this earth the center of the universe, when they had no conception of the vastness of interstellar space. We who have such conception know that this earth is but an insignificant speck, and it is, said Dr. Barnes, absurd to think that the redemption of man from his sins could possibly be the central interest of the God of the universe.

Many young people in college find their conceptions of God rudely shattered when they begin to study seriously some of the basic sciences, especially when they inquire into human behavior and hear some of the explanations of prayer so prevalent. They, like Dr. Barnes, confuse spiritual with spatial greatness. It has been asserted that the intelligence which centers in the mind of a single man has more significance than the largest galaxy now existing because if the galaxy were crushed out of existence it would know nothing of the process, but the man would *know* he was being crushed.

Spatial vastness cannot be computed or measured in the same terms as intelligence or spirit. Space and time are subservient to mind and purpose. So the science which deals with the discovery and apprehension of the divine mind—theology—is prior to and more important than any science dealing with the immensities of space—astrophysics. It is not the theologians but the undevout astronomer who errs when he scans in vain the handiwork of God for evidence of his existence. A faith in God which is for all practical purposes identical with a love for God must rule in the heart that seeks him. The person "that cometh to God, must *first* believe that he is, and that he is a rewarder of them that diligently seek him."

While the universe—God's handiwork—furnishes a source for the study of theology, its main source is found in the word of God, in the process of revelation and in the record of revelation.

Most of us have experienced breathtaking rapture

as we have listened for the first time to a great poem or symphony, or viewed a great statue, or gazed in concentrated peace upon a great masterpiece in oils. The experience lays hold on every part of us—heart, mind, and spirit. We apprehend beauty or we are apprehended by it. We are "caught up," so to speak, "lifted out of ourselves." Upon such occasions speech falters, and any statement of appreciation we may make is overruled by awe, wonder, and amazement. Something like worship ensues.

This same experience is true in the pursuit of truth. Rufus Jones tells how, while in college, he apprehended for the first time a great truth in the field of mathematics, and the apprehension so thrilled him that he ran the two miles to his home faster than ever before, leaping over obstacles he thought hitherto insurmountable for him. Thus the apprehension of truth, either in the realm of art or science, *liberates new power* in human life. In proportion to the quality of the work appreciated or the depth of the truth apprehended is the depth and power of our experience.

In this impact of the human mind upon these aspects of the universe true spiritual authority is exercised upon us. All authority resides in the nature of things as they are, as they were and as they are to come. The mind of man receives the flow of creative artistry or the impact of the divine mind, and he bows in rapture. He recognizes something akin to his own nature.

But this initial impact is only the beginning. Passive reception must issue in active acquisition.

The experience must be analyzed; the truth must be put to work. So a doctrine of art follows artistic experience. So canons of mathematics follow measurement and equation. So theology follows experience with God.

● ● ●

Our minds demand that our experience be organized and understood. So, after we have listened to a great symphony or poem we begin to ask questions: "Why does this symphony make me feel thus?" "How does the poet achieve the power to stretch my soul?" "By what magic is this artist more than a painter?" "How does he become a revealer?" Here the mental faculties begin to work on experience, and concepts of principles are fashioned. When this conceptual process is stated in propositional form, we have the *doctrine* of art.

But art is more than doctrine, just as revelation is more than truth about God...or just truth. But the work of art and its authoritative appeal precedes the statement or doctrine. Apprehension comes first. Comprehension follows when the mental faculties descry the principles upon which the artistic achievement is based. Comprehension dawns when meter and rhyme are discovered; or melodic line, movement of harmony, and key relation are disclosed; or when, in the case of a great painting, form and color consonance come to light. But the revelation itself is more than these.

A tone-deaf man may easily recite the principles of harmony, or a color-blind person state the doctrine of art, but his appreciation can never be complete. A map of Arizona will disclose the location of the Grand Canyon. Accurate direction as to how to get there can be obtained from the map. But because the map is an abstraction—a guide, and this alone—it can never convey the glory and beauty of the canyon itself. Doctrine is to revelation what the map is to the tourist. But the experience itself is more, inconceivably more, than the doctrine distilled from it.

Thus we are never content—unless we have diseased minds—to stay upon the second level of appreciation. Indeed, a distillation of doctrine from experience itself impels or inspires one to return to the experience with "freshened vision." With the principles clearly in mind, we return to the work of art. We look again, or we listen. A new grace comes. Again are we laid hold upon. This time our apprehension is infused with new meanings; it becomes understanding. We not only bow in his presence but have the mind of the artist, or the rudiments of it. The seed of artistry is in us. We have the prophecy of a capacity for similar creation.

Now we are in communion not only with the created thing but also with the mind of the creator. Revelation has its roots in the intercourse between mind and event. Always the event is the locus of revelation. The mind appreciates this. The prophets saw the movement of God in history. It was there before they saw it. Had they never apprehended it, it would still have been there, but it became revelation to them when they appreciated this divine movement.

What we have in the Old and New Testaments is not, therefore, revelation. It is a record made by the preceptor. It is, in the nature of things, a record of an interim experience between the first perception and the working out of what was perceived in the course of time. We cannot expect the divine self-disclosure to be made to us either in or out of the Scriptures, but through them. Theologians will analyze and summarize. Prophets will write "as they are moved upon by the Holy Ghost." But the theologian will turn from theology to worship, and the prophet will look up from the written page to contemplate the vision splendid and say,

> But great and marvelous are the
>   works of the Lord. . . .
> The whole earth is full of his glory.

There are, strictly speaking, no revealed truths. There are "truths of revelation"—statements of principles which stem from the actual revelatory experience. These may be, like the map, guides to the beatific vision—but they are not the vision itself. Revelation is based upon the intercourse between the mind which guides the event and the mind which views it. When an appreciation of Divinity in nature and history comes to man, revelation takes place.

We can easily see that the process of revelation, which conveys to us the mind of God, is the chief source of theology. Communion with the Creator will always issue in appreciation of that which he has created. Theology can thus be classed as a science, but a word must be said about the distinction between revelation and its record.

Sacred writings and formulated statements of doctrine are neither the substance nor the reality of revelation. They are records of the divine acts in which the revelation was given, or they are the formulated statement of faith. The purpose of scripture is to point the way by which men may find a renewal or a duplication of the experience which conveyed the nature of Deity. The object of the formulated statements of belief is God as revealed in Christ, and no sensible Christian worships either the Scriptures or the creeds.

Statements of belief are not themselves revelation but compilations of inferences drawn from living experience with God, the object of which is to bear testimony of that living experience and thus aid men to find a similar blessing. So, ever and always, the living Spirit of God is the guide and mentor of the theologian who recognizes that any present formulation of his faith or belief is not irrevocable, but such formulation needs constantly to be illumined and interpreted by the Spirit.

Most modern theology suffers from the fatal defect that marks every purely intellectual endeavor. Thought seems always to be in arrears of life, for we live first and think afterward. Thought runs on the surface of life. But life is deeper than thought. Therefore, when one tries to crowd into intellectual terms that which really lies deeper than thought, and which cannot be translated into grammar and syntax, the loss of meaning and power is really tremendous.

This is illustrated in the history of the early Christian Church. As soon as the church came to terms with the Empire—about A.D. 314—being passionately missionary, it sought to win the minds of the philosophers, professors of the schools and universities. These men were self-reliant and very independent. Even though the Emperor finally condemned paganism, these men remained aloof. They were sympathetic, it is true, but they would not accept Christianity until it could be presented in acceptable philosophical language. In trying to to do this, a process lasting over two hundred years, Christianity gradually and imperceptibly came to be a system to be believed rather than a life to be lived. The ancient symbols of that life, baptism and Eucharist, took on a sickly hue—"the pale cast of thought." And so the driving thrust of a pure moral life directed by the Spirit, which demanded the whole man to be effective, lost its force.

So it is always. People who cry for exact meanings of words, as the only tool by which life can be reshaped, miss the mark. The meaning of words is derived from their spiritual context, just as notes of a symphony combine with each other to convey the heart of the Master's message.

Theology thus must ever be baptized in worship and receive the gift of the Holy Ghost, and theologians must set their hands and hearts to do the will of God. Otherwise theology becomes a vain babel, and men think that thereby they can get to heaven simply by building towers with words and castles in the breath of their lips.

REVELATION

Does God actually speak to men today? Is it possible for us to have communion with him in such fashion as to make articulate to us his will and desire? This is a momentous question indeed, for if it is true that he does speak to men, then that is good news indeed.

Man shall not live by bread alone, we are told, but by every word that *proceedeth* out of the mouth of God. The verb here is present tense—not "has proceeded" or "will proceed" but every word that *proceedeth* out of the mouth of God. If this is true it takes for granted that there is such a Being who can fitly be called God, and that, moreover, he is personal. If this is so, then is there any consistent manifestation of his nature and purpose upon which men can build their lives—or is he completely hidden in this modern fantastic world of science and technology and completely obscured under the new morality about which we hear so much these days?

Most men long for secure foundations upon which they can plan their lives. They look for some voice of ultimate authority which can liberate them for constructive work. Can such foundations be discovered, or can such a voice be heard? The church teaches that it is possible for people to find the living God, and moreover, when they do they will find him speaking with the same steady voice of ultimate authority which has always characterized him.

The possibility of divine revelation rests in the nature of God. The Scriptures teach that he is personal; not, perhaps, that he is *a* person, but personal. He is probably personal in ways that we cannot imagine, combining in himself the realities which we glimpse in such scriptures as "which Father, Son and Holy Ghost are One God." He is the Creator, and being personal, such a One as to reveal himself, since communication is part of the essence of personality. Our notion of personality is limited by what we know of each other and of ourselves. But if we are to be rational and try to account for creation and ourselves, then God must be at least personal.

The worlds came into being by the Word of God. He spake and they were created, and into that which was thus formed he gave being. So then all is of God; it is a *form of his life*. And he never ceases to create, since he is Creator and this is his nature. Everything that has being and breath can thus be made to reveal him. "All things are created and made to bear record of me."

Only thus is science possible. All science could be, and "ought to be, a divine service, a reverent following of the traces of God's creation." What the scientist discovers are the actualizations of God's word. He may not recognize it as such, but if he seeks to know the truth, and not for some utilitarian purpose but because he loves the truth, then what he discovers is the word of God.

For creation means not only that God created but that he sustains his handiwork in being from moment to moment by ministering his life to it. He chose to create, and chooses to sustain creation. Therefore, the "book of Nature is the book of God."

What is true of nature is true also of human nature. History is a fit medium of divine revelation as is shown by the insight of the prophet. A divinely inspired event is seen by a divinely inspired mind and prophetic utterance is the result. Of course, none of the prophets were or are perfect and so the transmission of such insight is subject to some aberration. But in Jesus Christ, these aberrations are corrected and so he brings us the true interpretation of nature, man, and God.

If we try to articulate what the foregoing means in terms of divine revelation, we have to assert that all existence is a medium of revelation. The universe is sacramental. If this is not so, no particular revelation is possible. This is so because revelation depends upon the personal quality of that Ultimate Reality we call God. If there is no ultimate reality, then there is no God to be revealed; and if reality is not personal there can be no special or particular revelation—only uniform procedure, brute existence.

If God is, and if he is personal, then all existence can be made to reveal him. As Genesis says (6:66), "All things are created and made to bear record of me." Either all things and all occurrences are in some degree the revelation of the eternal God or else there is no such revelation at all. Those who affirm that revelation has ceased say that God is dead and deny his existence. And indeed to some, from their point of view, he is dead. What this really means is not that God is dead but that they are dead to him. The conditions of any revelation require that there should be nothing that is not revelation.

Only if God is revealed in the rising of the sun in the morning can he be revealed in the rising of his Son and all men from the dead. Only if he be revealed in the history of Russia can he be manifested in Palestine. Only if he is revealed in Europe can he be revealed in America, and in his church. In each case, of course, the manifestation is appropriate to the conditions obtaining. God must call all men or he cannot choose any man. Only if nothing is profane can anything be sacred. He must will that all become his sons, for if it were otherwise nobody could ever become his son.

And so we teach that the universe is sacramental. It can be made to show forth the living God. All things are thus created and made to bear record of him. Our constant prayer should be, "Open thou mine eyes, O Lord, that I may see the wondrous things out of thy law."

● ● ●

God is Creator and he is personal. We stress this at the outset because it is vital to our understanding of one of the principal doctrines and experiences of the church.

There are those who have substituted the idea

of causality for that of creation. This leads inevitably to the conclusion that the temporal universe is eternal, an idea which has vogue in many circles. One could trace every effect to its cause, which would be found to be the effect of something prior to it, and so on in endless regress.

Apart from the fact that it would be difficult to see how such a chain of cause and effect had its beginning, such a notion as the eternity of temporalities is inane. No meaning or purpose can be sensed in a vast never ending chain of cause and effect. Aristotle was keen enough to know this and postulated a First Cause, which itself was uncaused. H. G. Wells indicated that he could see no purpose or pattern to be found in the universe, and died in despair. Despair seems to be gripping more people than ever today, and the reason for this is that they, like Wells, can see no purpose in life and cry that there is nothing worth living for.

But if the universe is not eternal, then it was created. If created, then it has purpose or meaning incorporated in it—unless, of course, it was created by an idiot. If it has purpose, the universe is an expression of a personal will. There are some who believe that God *and* the world arise *together*, that he is the "principle of concreation," or that he is the "sum total of the values" to be found in the universe. For these people the universe and God exist together, and are mutually dependent. Dr. Alfred North Whitehead seems to hold to this view. But if this be true, then another ultimate reality has to be postulated to account for both God and the universe, "a God above God." But this line of thinking inevitably leads to the affirmation of a Being who created "out of nothing" that which we know as the world around us.

We are "deceivers, yet true" when we say God created the world, "Creation is a mythical idea which cannot be fully rationalized, said Reinhold Niebuhr. The philosophers have taken offense at it, and the scientists have substituted the notion of causality for it. Creation is a novel idea, and the origin of novelty is beyond our understanding, since everything we create is from the stuff of our own experience. The fact that the idea of creation is ultrarational does not make it untrue, but simply means that the notion has to be expressed in novel ways—hence the story in Genesis.

Why was creation undertaken? Moses asked this question and received the answer, "For mine own purpose have I made these things." All creative artists express *themselves* in what they create. The picture, the statue, the symphony are all expressions of the self. If they are true art they were brought into being primarily to please the artist, and so it is with the universe and man in it. God created it to please him, not us. He created us to please him, and undertook his work that sometime somewhere he might discover himself reflected in what he made. He created us as persons upon whom he could lavish his love.

We may ask, "Before all worlds, was God love? If so, how was that love expressed, and toward whom?" If God is love, and also eternal, then love is eternal. If he is almighty, and love, then love is almighty.

The answer to this question has always been that God loved his Son, who was "begotten before all worlds." God loves his Son, the Word. Eternally this is so. It was out of this love, dwelling eternally in him, that he created. For, "we heard the voice bearing record that he [Christ] is the Only Begotten of the Father; that by him, and through him, and of him, the worlds are and were created; and the inhabitants thereof are begotten sons and daughters unto God."

Behind the outer visible world there is reality which is invisible and eternal. We know this because very often we are in the grip of a sublime sense of something "far more deeply interfused whose dwelling is the light of setting suns." And we exclaim with the poet, "How exquisitely is the mind fitted to the external world, and the external world to the mind." With Paul of old, we look not at the things which are seen, but at the things which are not seen; "for the things which are not seen are eternal."

We can understand this amazing language only if we recognize that the universe is a process. It is a living thing which is on its way somewhere, so to speak. We cannot imagine the ancient apostle holding to the notion that there was a necessary antagonism between temporal and spiritual. There is no antagonism between them. All we see and hear and sense in our relation to the world around us is but an episode in an eternal program which had its origin in God and which will eventually come to rest in him. We are told that the heavens and the earth shall pass away and as they do a new heaven and a new earth shall replace them. But of his word it is said, "My word shall not pass away," but shall accomplish the end whereunto it was sent.

The men of science confirm this view that the universe is fundamentally spiritual. Matter and light, mass and energy are but different forms manifesting the same reality. In this connection we quote Sir James Jeans who wrote in his book, *The Mysterious Universe:* "The whole physical universe is composed of waves [radiation]. The bottled waves we call matter, and the unbottled waves we call light, so that the whole process of creation may be adequately summarized in the six words in the book of Genesis, 'God said, Let there be light.'" How marvelously thus does science support the divine word! "And the light which now shineth, which giveth you light, is through him who en-lighteneth your eyes, which is the same light that quickeneth your understandings; which light pro-ceedeth forth from the presence of God, to fill the immensity of space. The light which is in all things; which giveth life to all things; which is the law by which all things are governed; even the power of God who sitteth upon his throne, who is in the bosom of eternity, who is in the midst of all things."

The light which "proceedeth forth from the presence of God to fill the immensity of space" constitutes the governing law which holds the physical universe in its grip, controls its behavior, and determines its spheres of usefulness. Even so, the light of the sun which appears to be the origin of all physical phenomena is itself but a shadow of a greater and far more significant light—the light of the Spirit. Sunlight, in other words, is a phase of the ministry of the Holy Spirit.

Dean Inge has written, "Creation is a hymn sung by the creative Logos, to the glory of God."

Revelation is much more than a mere human experience. Moses did not meet God and talk with him "face-to-face" *in the same way* that we might meet and converse with another human being—a friend. The human side of the experience is truly part of what happens when God and man meet, but it is only a part.

Michelangelo's "Moses" is infinitely much more than the stone in which it is carved. It is quite true, of course, that the stone is a necessary element in the artistic experience, even as the human side of the revelatory experience is necessary. A manifestation that did not reflect a human experience would be like a statue carved in the wind. But the event of revelation must never be fully equated with men's experience of it. The word "revelation" is simply indicative of a sublimity far beyond the mere symbol. So the human record of revelation which is constituted in the divine-human encounter indicates a glory far beyond the word.

"Behold," the Lord says to Moses, "I reveal unto you concerning this heaven and this earth." This is far different from what happens when an astronomer says, "Let me tell you about the heavens," or when a geologist offers to "tell you about the earth." The words spoken by the geologist and the astronomer are physical-psychological facts. The words of God, however, enshrine a great mystery. They come from his Being. The record which issues from a revelatory experience is designed to evoke wonder, admiration, and awe.

The movement of God toward man, God seeking after him, is wholly irreducible to verbal definition and is utterly beyond the powers of our comprehension. It is beyond our imagination—except imagination be quickened by the God who reveals himself. Only he who has experienced it knows how it happens, and the words he uses to describe the experience or record the process are simply tools designed to prompt and inspire a like experience in those who hear them.

The confrontation between God and Elijah (I Kings 19:11, 12) indicates, by a series of negatives, the area in which Elijah was apprehended by the Creator.

> Go forth and stand upon the mount before the Lord.
> And, behold the Lord passed by.
> And a great strong wind rent the mountains,
> And broke in pieces the rocks before the Lord;
> But the Lord was not in the wind;
> And after the wind, an earthquake;
> But the Lord was not in the earthquake;
> And after the earthquake, a fire;
> But the Lord was not in the fire;
> And after the fire, a still small voice.

It was only after hearing the "Voice of silence" that Elijah, a passionate and fiery servant of the Lord, wrapped his face in his mantle and went to the mouth of the cave to listen.

We are utterly inadequate in mind to describe

the Eternal. The same applies to his revelation of himself. When we attempt to describe or define the experience it eludes us.

With these preliminary remarks about the nature of revelation we must add the dictum that although revelation and its process remain something of a mystery to us, it is none the less real. God did and does make his will known to man now as formerly. While we cannot contain a full understanding of the process in our trite minds, yet it is incontrovertible that the process exists. It exists and is beyond reason, while it displays a wisdom all its own.

It is not only with his eyes that man sees, nor with his ears alone that man hears. Knowledge of the temporal world is delivered to man through the five senses. But the spiritual faculties, when quickened by the Spirit of God, apprehend that all temporal existence mirrors a great mystery. All human thought and all objects of all thought are vessels of the ineffable. Something far more beautiful and far more terrible than we can imagine is at the heart of reality.

We may thank God that we apprehend this fact, for apprehension of this is the beginning of divine wisdom. It is the connection between God and man upon which is based the possibility of revelation. But God cannot speak and convey his beauty if there is no idea in man that the mystery exists.

Here is the utter inadequacy of modern man. He never stops to ask the question as to whether God speaks today. He does not trouble himself that God spoke to Moses or was revealed in Jesus

Christ. This he takes for granted and promptly forgets about it. Modern man has no problem in relation to what God demands of him. He listens to every self-centered voice but the voice of God.

This is the tragedy of modern life, because revelation has the answer to every human and social problem. But men cannot ask the right questions anymore. They feel themselves either so self-sufficient as to need no guidance or else so insignificant as to be unworthy of the divine notice or so ignorant they do not care. Pride and false humility characterize our age. Both attitudes are damnable. They blind men to the realities to which the prophets and our Lord Jesus Christ all testified.

Years ago it was thought that social reforms would eliminate all ills from the world. We have since learned at great cost that bread and power cannot save us from ourselves. There is a disposition to "hurt and destroy" in the soul of man that can be cast out only through the fear of God. Man is suffocating in selfishness, and only the love and power of God can help him breathe.

The process of revelation, we have said, is a mystery. It must always be so to some extent since revelation is an *act in the life of God* as well as an event in the life of man. And who shall say what the life of God is? The mystics have tried to answer this question. Mysticism is a quest for esoteric experience. The mystic rejoices when he has attained the goal he longs for—namely, the beatific vision. But not so the prophet. He does not relish what he apprehends. Although the experience may be "sweet in his mouth," it is "bitter in his belly." Revelation is not what he seeks after, *but the result of his being sought after by God.*

The history of Israel illustrates this, and it is reflected in the church today. It is God's perpetual search after man that is the main event in the life of the Restoration church (the church which is modern Israel). God is not a detached overlord whom we seek after. He is the living vital soul in the heart of all, and he seeks after and even at times "pursues" us. But when we seek him it is only after we are commanded and prompted to do so, and our seeking is a result of his seeking us. And it may truly be said that he who seeks after God has already found him.

"The way *to* God is a way *of* God" (Heschel). God could never be revealed to us unless he himself had first sought after us. Before we ever knew we needed him, he wanted us for himself.

As Augustine has said: "Thou hast made us for thyself, and our souls are restless until they rest in thee."

● ● ●

The important fact in the revelatory experience is not that man hears, but that God speaks. The prophet to whom his will is conveyed is caught up into the life of the Divine.

In an authentic religious experience there is an element of the "numinous." Professor Otto in his book, *The Idea of the Holy*, has called attention to what he calls "numinous" in religious experience.

By this we mean that when men feel they have encountered the Divine they experience a feeling of awe, coupled with a feeling of irresistible attraction, or "creature feeling," which fascinates them while it draws and holds them spellbound.

This is reflected in the early history of Israel. In this, one may note the almost shuddering dread with which God was approached. "A dread and great darkness" was upon Abraham (Genesis 15:12), seraphim covered their faces, and Isaiah cries, "I am undone" (Isaiah 6:5). One may liken the bush Moses saw burning while yet it was not consumed in the fire to Mount Sinai which was not melted, or to Israel which was not annihilated. When God uttered his word, "Mount Sinai was wrapped in smoke, because the Lord descended upon it in a fire. The smoke of it went up like the smoke of a kiln, the whole mountain trembled greatly" (Exodus 19:18). "The mountain burned with fire to the heart of heaven, with darkness, clouds, and thick darkness" (Deuteronomy 4:11). The mountain burned with fire and was not consumed. Here is a new dimension in man's apprehension of God— namely a fire that did not consume. Yet at Sinai the people shuddered at the thought of a divine theophany. To Moses they said, "Speak thou with us, and we will hear; but let not God speak to us lest we die" (Exodus 20:19).

And so when the temple was built a veil separated the sanctuary from the holy of holies, signifying that a great mystery stands between God and the people. They are overawed. They tremble and stand a great way off.

40

But within the mystery there is a voice. In the midst of deep darkness there is a great light. So the psalmist can say, "The Lord reigns; let the earth rejoice; let many coastlands be glad. Clouds and deep darkness are round about him; righteousness and justice are the foundations of his throne" (Psalm 97:1, 2). Joseph Smith utters language in consonance with this: "Hear, O ye heavens, and give ear, O earth,...for the Lord is God, and beside him there is no Savior; great is his wisdom; marvelous are his ways; and the extent of his doings, none can find out" (Doctrine and Covenants 76:1). Over and above the mystery there is meaning; in the midst of it there is light. Revelation is a process involving both God and man, by which the veil is taken away and some of the meaning vouchsafed. In Jesus Christ the mystery is penetrated. In him the veil of the temple is rent. In him God stands revealed as far as man can reveal him.

How shall we apprehend God? How can one man really understand another except he be like him, or else he cultivate to a great degree the spirit of sympathetic imagination by which he is able to put himself in the other man's position and look at the world through his eyes? Knowledge of lower forms of life demands that the knower take the initiative in the process of knowing. The higher the order of life the more demanding the discipline. In knowing another person the initiative does not rely solely upon the one who would know, but partly on the person he desires to know. The initiative in human relationships is cut in half.

All of us who enjoy rich and meaningful friendships know that our knowledge of each other is a reciprocal process. If my friend decides to sever this reciprocity, to shut himself away from me, there is not very much I can do about it.

To know the Lord Jesus, however, who is God manifest in the flesh, requires that the initiative in the process of knowing him rests wholly on his side. Only if he shall reveal himself to us can we know him. And even when he reveals himself there is always the hazard that in taking the revelation we may *mis*-take it. Principles enunciated by him can very easily be, and often are, subject to human interpretation. Even the record of past revelation can be taken by an evil man to further his evil ends. This is illustrated in the great temptation of our Lord when the devil quoted the record of Moses to support an invitation he offered to the Savior. How then can we know him? How can he reveal himself to us?

The study of history offers us some help. Men of excellent scholarship and saintly life have written about the background of the life and times of Jesus. We owe a debt of gratitude to them. In these works many of the sayings and doings of our Lord come to light, and we are blessed with insights which are extremely helpful.

In this relation one is reminded of the injunction to "seek learning by study and also by faith" and to "study all good books." Through this exercise one may apprehend principles of conduct and so be helped tremendously in his spiritual life. But at best this exercise gives us only knowledge *about* Jesus Christ. We do not know him fully in this way.

Saul of Tarsus knew the Master "after the manner of men." As long as he knew him only in this way his knowledge was not inconsistent with his persecution of the members of the church. Always the knowledge of the Master which is communicated by someone else is subject to aberration and some error. We rejoice in the reflected light that comes to us through these men of learning and wisdom, yet long for the fuller revelation he makes to "those that wait with him alone." Here we come to the heart of the matter.

Only Jesus Christ himself can tell us who he is. Only Christ himself can tell us what he will do. Only Christ himself can tell us what he would have us do. If our knowledge of him rests upon a revealment given long, long ago, and left to the interpretation of others, be they ever so saintly, our knowledge will grow dim and ever dimmer with the passing of the years. And as our knowledge of him grows dim, so wanes our power over ourselves. Our ability to control our lusts and evil desires also grows less and less.

This is shown in two ways. Modern theology is in a welter of indecision. A name comes to the fore, a man dominates the "thinking" of many people for years, and then there arises another, with a different point of view. Ever learning are they, and they never come to a knowledge of the truth. Argument succeeds argument as to the exact meaning of the "Word" of Scripture, and no one ever really succeeds in revealing the mysteries of the kingdom. The other way in which this is shown is in the growing godlessness of our generation. It is coming to pass with each succeeding day that "Evil men and seducers shall wax worse and worse, for men shall be lovers of their own selves, proud, highminded." The lack of knowledge of the Lord Jesus, that knowledge imparted to man by and through himself, has issued in moral and spiritual decay. The cause is outlined to us in modern revelation. It is because "Every man walketh in his own way, after the image of his own god, whose image is in the likeness of the world, and whose substance is that of an idol!"

Idols have a way of becoming old and outmoded. Not so the revelation in Christ. Let us seek him ever and always.

● ● ●

Our heavenly Father has prepared many books wherein we may read of his dealings with men. One of these books tells of his revelation to the poets and prophets of Israel and culminates in the life and death and resurrection of Jesus Christ the Righteous. To this book, or rather this collection of books, we give the name The Holy Scriptures. This church holds in high affection two other books which contain records of the revelations of God to men, the Book of Mormon and the Book of Doctrine and Covenants. But God has not confined his revelation of himself to these books alone. There are other books wherein the story of his love and goodness is written for our profit.

Nature, which the poet Cowper has said to be "but a name for an effect whose cause is God," is one of these books, written by the hand of God himself. We cannot yet read the bible of Nature as we hope to do. Indeed, we can as yet spell out only a few halting phrases. But we can there read enough to fire our minds with the glory and the wonder of what is not yet understood.

"Put off thy shoes from off thy feet, for the place whereon thou standest is holy ground—this should be the attitude of the soul by the sounding sea, or on the solid hill, or in the rejoicing wood. Feel the musical soul of divine thought and love which is moving everywhere; pass with hallowed awe and joy into the artistry of God revealed in, and making, the outward world."

The word of Jesus is even more suggestive. Consider it: "Why take ye thought for raiment? Consider the lilies of the field, how they grow; they toil not, neither do they spin; and yet I say unto you, that even Solomon in all his glory was not arrayed like one of these. Wherefore if God so clothe the grass of the field, which today is, and tomorrow is cast into the oven, shall he not much more clothe you, if ye are not of little faith?"

The outburst of flowers in the spring of Palestine is uncertain and short lived. The poppies, daisies, and anemones and the fresh green of the grass have disappeared before the end of May and might well suggest the obvious parallel of the brevity of human life. Is it not a higher and deeper lesson which Jesus draws? The flowers come every

year and are very soon withered, yet God thinks
it is worthwhile to make them beautiful. Will he
do less for us? Does not their existence reveal
his creative artistry, and does not his care for
them justify us in anticipating an even greater
care for us? Is there not here a revelation of
Divinity which should both stir and warm our hearts?

Our Father, who has revealed himself in nature,
has also left the evidences of his own nature and
purpose in history and in literature. The hand of
God has evidently been over the nations for their
good, and his influence on the destinies of men
can be traced by persons of information and
discernment. His goodwill toward all men is clearly
revealed, for example, in the culmination of
knowledge and invention in many wonders which
will undoubtedly promote human brotherhood when
they are controlled by men of goodwill.

But the clearest revelation of Divinity comes to
the common man through other men whose lives
have been devoted to the worship of God. Our
Father reveals himself through persons in proportion
to the depth and power of their religious experiences.
In the life of Jesus, that inflow of Divinity was
perfectly unhindered, and the life of the Master
was in consequence the supreme revelation of God
to man. "No one knoweth the Father save the Son,
and he to whomsoever the Son willeth to reveal
him." And it is not the wise and understanding to
whom the Son wills to make this revelation, but
the "babes." It was because Jesus was himself
the perfect embodiment of the child spirit that the
truth of God became luminous in him, and it is

only as we come to share the spirit of simplicity, teachableness, and obedience that he can reveal truth to us. In the words of Edward Grubb: "Revelation is the manifestation of the character or quality of God, the perfect person, through persons; and most of all through the one person who has lived the perfect life."

The record of what God has said to others is very important. We must be grateful for it. But if he loves men why should he not speak as well today as in former times? Is it completely wise that we remain forever content with what others have said about Jesus, or what he has said to them? Why should he not talk to us? Is the difficulty that we do not expect enough— that we are content with too little? Perhaps it is.

We cannot be content with what others say about Christ. "Every man should speak in the name of the Lord, even the Savior of the world."

What is most desperately needed, both in the world and in the church, is that everyone should know the Lord for himself. Moses once said, "Would to God all God's people were prophets and that the Lord would put his Spirit upon them."

Here is the key to the understanding of Jesus Christ: It is the Spirit of God, in the Holy Ghost, whose function it is to reveal the Father and the Son. There is no substitute for this. Scholarship alone cannot bring men into the presence of the Master so that there occurs that personal confrontation which is the essence of the revelatory experience. This is not to deride scholarship. Scholarship is like enriching the soil, but enriching the soil does not plant the seed. Enriching the mind does not alone bring that intercourse between God and man which we have tried to describe as necessary to the full revelation of the Master and his kingdom.

Revelation is a process which outruns reason, and reaches into the very depths of man's nature. Scholarship may enlighten. Revelation redeems. Scholarship may impart knowledge about Jesus. Revelation gives him to men. Appreciation may be enlarged and enriched through disciplined study, but only the Holy Ghost can engrave in man's soul the image of the invisible God who is Jesus Christ. Contemplation of the beauty and the wonder of that one perfect life is doubtless a profitable experience. Many of us are too busy to cultivate the art of meditation. But only the Spirit of God can convey the motives of the kingdom and help us to possess the loves that characterize the eternal God.

Revelation, then, in its larger aspects, always conveys a heaven-sent gift. It is not merely the enlightenment of mind, although this is included. It is not simply the enrichment of the artistic nature nor the strengthening of the will to righteousness, although these are comprehended in the revelatory experience. It is new being.

"Except a man be born again, he cannot see.... And except he be born of the water and of the Spirit he cannot enter...." Men have to be, before they can become.

● ● ●

The prophets of Israel left with mankind the idea that God was utterly righteous and that he was holy. This, when intellectually considered, is ethical monotheism. But ethical monotheism was not an inference from experience. It grew out of illumination which arose in communion with God. It had to do with conscience rather than with intellect, although it had intellectual implications. The prophets adored the great "I AM" and in the light of their adoration they read the signs of their times and beyond. So Abraham exclaims in wonder. "Shall not the Judge of all the earth do right?"

Our response to God is drawn from us by acts which are objectively displayed before us. God utters himself in his Word, which bodies forth the universe. We who are parts of the universe respond to that Word, in whatever measure our sense of appreciation moves us. When that Word is presented to us in the person of Jesus through the Holy Spirit, the response enkindled is a revelation of that Spirit. And the only appropriate response to such revealment in Christ is gratitude which issues in love of him. And so Jesus asked Peter the question, "Lovest thou me?" Peter's response is well known. But the significant fact is that Christ made Peter's love for him to be the mainspring of ministry. It is only through the revelation of the Lord Jesus to us by and of himself that we find the power to have charity for each other. Charity is the fruitage of the revelation of Jesus Christ. Charity is the wellspring of ministry.

We may hear for the first time a great symphony, experience the awe and beauty of it, and allow the sweet concourses of sound to sweep over our souls. Then we are in the presence of something sublime. The experience lifts us out of ourselves. Our critical faculties are hushed and still. We are held spellbound. But then our appreciation of the music will be heightened by a study of the score, or by knowledge of the circumstances which occasioned its writing, or by a knowledge of the life of the composer—who he is, where he came from. In this connection we add to our original experience the perceptions which come from analysis, or an intellectual penetration of our experience. From such exercise we derive certain doctrine about the music as to style, key relationships, and characteristic rhythms. But if we stop there, and never go back again to the hearing of the music, this time with what the intellect has given us, we abort the whole function of music itself. The intellectual exercise is very beneficial, but if it stops there it does us little good. If we go back again and listen once more, or ten times more, how much greater the ministry we receive from the composer!

The same principle applies to revelation. Once experience with God is sustained, certain truths about the experience may be distilled from it. But this process of distilling truth from revelation is only an interim procedure. Unless it leads to and induces us to further seek and trust God, it is abortive. A doctrine about revelation is not revelation. Truths distilled from revelation may provide the basis for intellectual and philosophical exercise, which as far as it goes is good. But unless such intellectual procedure induces us to worship God in the beauty of holiness it does not help very much. In fact it can become a positive hindrance if there is substituted a love of the doctrine for the love of God. There are no divinely communicated doctrines as such. There are truths of revelation. These may be expressed in propositions which are the result of correct thinking about revelation, but they are neither themselves that revelation nor are they directly revealed. God is always more than our thoughts of him, although it is wise that we think about him correctly. Always the theologian must correct his ideas in worship else his ideas may crystallize, crack, and crumble away.

The fatal substitution of the processes of the intellect divorced from the whole being of man is seen in the following, written by Dr. Pringle-Pattison:

> In every religion the question at issue is the character of its God or Gods; for on that depends its whole conception of human duty and its view of human destiny. The lesson of Christianity is that we have to think of God in terms of Christ...in terms, that is to say, of his recorded teaching and of the spirit of his dedicated life and death. And in order to give us authentic tidings of the character of God, Jesus did not require actually to *be* God.

This passage betrays a devotion to conceptual thinking which is illustrative of the contention we have asserted. It falls quite short of the truth. "Tidings of the character of God" are such propositions about him as can be conveyed in speech, and it is not incompatible with the suggestion that Jesus did not need actually to *be* God to convey the "values" of God to us. But what we need to know is, can we trust our lives to this Jesus as we would to the eternal God? No intellectual description of Jesus or what he represented is capable of leading us to this trust. Anyone who has known the Lord Jesus, or who does now know him, has no doubt as to his identity. He was and is God. "Show us the Father," said Philip, "and it sufficeth us." The rejoinder given by Christ is eloquent: "Have I been so long time with you, Philip, and yet hast thou not known me?"

Correct thought about Christ, the ultimate revelation of God in an individual, is highly desirable, but unless it leads us into his presence so that we worship, it is abortive. It is only in worship when spirit communicates with Spirit that the life of God passes into the soul of man. This kind of communion is the whole purpose and object of the process of revelation.

If we are to know God, it must be by revelation, that is, by an inward light that shines in our own souls and which is not the mere result of sense experience or intellectual demonstration. While all these things may have their right and necessary place in preparing us in the knowledge of God they cannot give conviction by themselves. This assurance is given of God and is promised to those who seek him. Thus John the Revelator is reminded, "If any man hear my voice, and open the door, I will come unto him, and sup with him, and he with me" (Revelation 3:20).

Men need God and seek after him, and because they believe he has been found in days past, succeeding generations go out more confidently in quest of him. But the experience of the righteous when their search is rewarded is that he was first seeking after them. Our self-will impedes our discovery of God. That is why prayer is so important in the Christian experience, for it is the chief agency by which self-will is overcome and channels are opened for Divinity to come into our lives. Prayer is not designed to change the will of God; its purpose is that we may lay our will alongside his and so bring him and his purpose into our lives. We do not attempt to alter his will to suit our desire but to adjust our desire to his will.

This is what Jesus meant when he reminded his disciples that "the pure in heart shall see God." Only those who love him and keep his commandments can ever truly "know" him (John 14:21). The gospel of John is packed full of the thought that the light of God has been shed forth in the hearts of men, and that as they obey and follow this light, they are led to receive the fuller light which shines in "the word made flesh" (John 1:4, 9; 3:19, 20; 5:17; 6:44, 45; 12:32, etc.). This, too, is the teaching of modern revelation:

The light shineth in darkness, and the darkness comprehendeth it not; nevertheless, the day shall come when you shall comprehend even God; being quickened in him, and by him. Then shall ye know that ye have seen me, that I am, and that I am the true light that is in you, and that you are in me, otherwise ye could not abound.—Doctrine and Covenants 85:12 e, f.

This is what Paul meant when he said that "the natural man receiveth not the things of the Spirit of God" because they are to be "spiritually discerned" (I Corinthians 2:14).

Revelation is a gift of God made possible by his expanding life in the souls of men. As our eyelids open to the daylight our knowledge of truth is always growing, and our humility grows with a consciousness that the gifts of insight and revelation and understanding have always been waiting for us, but that the way of life has been barricaded by our own blindness and hardness of heart. God has taken the initiative for our redemption. As we move toward him we find him already hastening toward us.

● ● ●

It has been our contention that revelation is actually more than our apprehension or record of it. It is an event in the life of God as well as an experience in the life of man. In the revelatory experience nature is visited by a power that is above and beyond nature, in a different and far more glorious dimension than we can apprehend. There is no continuity between things natural and things spiritual. Between them there is a gulf fixed. "That which is born of the flesh, *is* flesh. . . .No man can ascend to heaven. . . ."

But the gulf has been bridged by the spiritual reaching down into the natural. In this process the natural becomes imbued and endowed with a glory which is beyond the natural, and the natural becomes transformed into new dimensions. The treasure is held in earthen vessels, but the vessels in which it is held are and remain earthen. The words (earthen vessels) which enshrine revelation can convey that revelation only as the Spirit which indites them is received into the mind and heart of him who reads or listens. Perhaps we can make the meaning clear if we can find in the natural realm instances where a higher form is transposed into a lower medium of expression.

Liszt transposed the nine symphonies of Beethoven for the piano. Thus a higher form was transposed into a lower medium. The symphony orchestra is composed of four different choirs—strings, woodwinds, brass, and percussion. The sound produced by the striking of a piano key is like none of them. Therefore, each note on the piano has to stand for four different sounds, and if the symphony score duplicates or triples the tone on any note to reinforce or produce richer overtones, then the piano string has to stand for these too.

Imagine, if you will, a country where nobody ever heard or saw a symphony orchestra, and into which a piano was introduced. On it would be played one of these Liszt transcriptions of a symphony. Could the people who heard it imagine what the symphony of which it was a transcription really sounded like? Their appreciation would be limited by the medium into which it was cast. It would be rich, perhaps, as it was, but infinitely poorer than the music of which it was representative. It is impossible to put into a piano transcription exactly what a symphony is. But a person who is familiar with the work as a whole, and hears the symphony repeatedly, appreciates the piano version in a far greater measure than one who has never heard it.

There is a word of God, and there is a word of man, into which the word of God is transposed.

When the word of God is transposed into a word of man, there is always something of infinite value lost in the process. One may hear the word of man, or see the record of revelation and read it, but unless he hears the Word of God through the word of man there is no complete revelation of the Divine.

The organ through which the divine revelation is expressed is the whole man. But the elements in the human nature must stand for more than they themselves are, just as the notes on the piano. In the process of communication between God and man, our heavenly Father must transpose that which he has to give us into a lower order of life. The transposition was as perfect as man could make it in Jesus. Insofar as man can reveal God, Jesus so revealed him. But there is beyond even this an infinite glory which will take us, with a glorified nature, the whole of eternity to apprehend—if those words have any meaning. So Jesus at the end of his earthly life asked simply, "Glorify me now with the glory I had with thee before the world was." Human nature, body and spirit together, are unable fully to reveal the ultimate glory. "Flesh and blood cannot inherit the kingdom of God."

In view of the foregoing it is no wonder that those who have glimpsed the celestial realm can find no words adequately to express the experience. And so Joseph Smith records:

But great and marvelous are the works of the Lord and the mysteries of his kingdom which he showed unto us, which surpasses all understanding in glory, and in might, and in dominion, which he commanded us we should not write, while we were yet in the Spirit, and are not lawful for man to utter, neither is man capable to make them known, for they are only to be seen and understood by the power of the Holy Spirit.—Doctrine and Covenants 76:8a, b.

It is well to observe also that when the attempt is made to transpose the higher into the lower the best the lower has to offer is inadequate. And so, when John saw into the divine kingdom (Revelation), he could talk only about thrones, crowns, jewels, gold, and precious stones. This is not only true in words; it is true also of symbolic action. In the sacrament of the Lord's Supper the worshipers are united with Christ in an act of mystical communion. But from another point of view Eucharist is only eating and drinking. If we approach transposition from the lower level, we shall not apprehend the higher. But if we have experienced the higher realm, then what the lower medium becomes is a channel or vehicle into which the higher is poured and in which it is revealed.

Every human faculty, when man is endowed with the divine Spirit, is enhanced and quickened. Intellect, will, emotion are made representative of something beyond themselves. All thought appears to be accompanied by impulses in the brain which can be measured on an encephalograph. But is this all there is to thought? Does the measurement of the responses in the brain indicate the quality of thought in which we are engaged? Does, then, the brain secrete thought much as the liver secretes bile? If one turns from an experience of intense aesthetic rapture and by introspection tries to catch what is happening, all he can do is to tabulate a physical sensation. Then is all music appreciation merely physical sensation?

We may well ask, What is the connecting link between natural and spiritual, temporal and eternal, this world and the kingdom? The answer is "faith." Faith is the nexus between God and man. "He that cometh to God *must* first believe that he is, and that he is a rewarder of them that diligently seek him. But without faith it is impossible to please God." The apostle here recognizes that the ultimate spiritual reality is connected to areas of the human soul which lie deeper than the intellect.

We begin our lives in this world in a cradle of love. "Heaven lies around us in our infancy." The child trusts his parents. That trust is the natural response to love. Love calls it forth and blesses its expression. This is analogous to the spiritual world. We are begotten through Jesus Christ into a "living hope." Our response to such activity on the part of the Creator is faith and trust in him. Love always calls forth trust. How often Jesus admonished his disciples to "have faith in God."

Through faith God is able to transpose his intelligence, and vouchsafe to us something of his eternal glory. But without faith shall "nothing be shown forth except desolations upon Babylon." "Behold the days have come when according to men's faith it shall be done unto them."

• • •

We affirm that God *IS* and that in him perfect love and absolute power are one and the same thing.

Perfect love is ultimate power. We are used to the possession of power. With it we move mountains and change rivers from their courses. We have tamed the lightning and harnessed the wind.

But such power as we know and have is not to be compared to that which the Creator wielded when he said, "Let there be light." The word of God is quick and powerful, sharper than a two-edged sword, to the dividing asunder of both joints and marrow—soul and spirit. It is also a discerner of the thoughts and intents of the heart. God utters his voice and what he says happens. There is no power like this.

But that same God, who thus uttered his voice, one day found himself bowed to the earth and sweating great drops of blood, saying, "Father, if it be possible, let this cup pass from me; nevertheless, not what I will, but what thou wilt!" Wherein resided the difference between uttering his voice and having it obeyed, and finding himself frustrated and confused?

The difference lay in the power required to make a universe, and the power needed to change the stony heart of a wicked man into a loving one. "Let there be light!" There is no apparent effort here. But to reach into our lives and win our hearts' allegiance requires the death of the cross. God is entirely adequate in the display of his power to do both. And ultimately the two kinds of power are one. We may be overpowered and mastered and so made to conform by the display of naked elemental force; but only love and sacrifice can win our hearts' allegiance. The God of absolute power is as humble as a little child. It is very difficult for us to realize this, and far more difficult to practice it.

The God in whom absolute power and perfect love dwell together is far removed from the God of modern existentialism. The existentialist says, "God exists for me to the degree in which I, in freedom, authentically become myself. He does not exist as a scientific content, but only as an openness to existence." So asserts Karl Jaspers, who is a fairly representative spokesman. But what does he mean? Can his words mean anything? What is the difference between this and sheer subjectivism?

Jean Paul Sartre, another existentialist, tells us he too seeks to become authentically himself. But he is an avowed atheist. He asserts that because God does not exist, his freedom is his own. One cannot but admire the attitude which takes full responsibility for one being and doing what he is and does. We all tend to stand a little taller and straighter when Sartre tells us we ought to take responsibility for our own lives. But if God does not exist, we are left to the worship of whatever image of ourselves we, in our freedom, make. Again, if he does exist, and is above us and our concepts so far as to be inaccessible—in other words, if there is a God above God of whom we know nothing—we are left only with the courage to be whatever we have imagined to ourselves.

One may conceive an ideal self as far as he is able, and eternally assert this to himself, but he will never lose the conviction that he is creating

60

his own god. After all, this is the age-old sin, that we continually seek to become gods to ourselves. Existentialism has no basis for a universal and ultimate faith.

But God does exist. He has come to us in the revelation of himself in his Son. That revelation is made alive in the operation of his Spirit. Whether anyone in the universe ever acknowledged him or not he would still be! This conviction is vital to a sane faith.

This is illustrated in the following. A young woman once asked Dr. Jowett: "O Master, tell me, what do you think about God?" The great man replied: "That, my dear young lady, is a very unimportant question. The only thing that signifies is what he thinks about me!" This showed that Dr. Jowett believed in the objective existence of God, the great Subject, who claimed Jowett for himself.

In the consciousness of such objectivity exists the possibility of fellowship. As far as we are mutually concerned with the object of our faith we are drawn together and find fellowship. We have a common interest. A man devoted to the truth always rejoices with and in those who make advances in knowledge. But if a scientist or a saint is primarily concerned with his own reputation and makes love of truth an accessory to this, he will be jealous of all those who make discoveries. So will the fellowship among scientists be disrupted. So will the fraternity among members of the church be jeopardized. As long as we are mainly concerned about God and his service we have fellowship with each other. We are happy in each others' achievements. But if we become unduly concerned with our own spiritual state or status, or our reputation, then we become occupied with what is ours distinctively and so separate ourselves one from the other, and fall eventually into antagonism.

In science the way to the truth or salvation demands that a man forget himself and concentrate all his faculties upon his object. The greatest achievement of the human mind in the nineteenth century was the discovery of Neptune. The search for the truth leaped over individual and national boundaries and found an Englishman, a Frenchman, and a German working together excitedly, forgetting utterly their national origin in the eager joy of anticipated discovery.

So it should be with us in our spiritual life. Each has a particular and specific angle of vision which, if used rightly, will enable him to discover just that aspect of the divine beauty the constitution of his mind qualifies him to apprehend and appreciate. That is the way of salvation.

Our faith must be universal and ultimate. All our experience should be related to God who makes us and our experience possible. It should lead us to self-forgetfulness in the unremitting pursuit of the Divine through all our lives.

Only as each does this, and only as we do this together, will the church be lifted out of obscurity.

● ● ●

A Hebrew prophet who lived long ago said, "This is the generation of them that seek him; that seek thy face, O Jacob." What he said long ago is true now. Every generation seeks after God, if haply they may find him. It is in the constitution of man's nature to do this.

C. S. Lewis has said:

God made us; invented us as a man invents an engine. A car is made to run on gasoline, and it would not run properly on anything else. Now God designed the human machine to run on Himself. He, Himself, is the fuel our spirits are designed to burn, or the food our spirits were designed to feed on. There is no other.

And so it was that Jesus gave us the first commandment, to "love the Lord thy God with all thy heart, might, mind and strength." And it was a commandment, not a piece of philosophy. Men ought to love God first, for he is the life of their lives. Man's deepest need is for God, and because of this every generation seeks after him.

H. R. MacIntosh wrote:

Whenever men take to heart their own destiny, as well as the destiny of those to whom they are linked by ties of home and fatherland and humanity, they uniformly reveal a longing for the unseen, and for the fellowship therewith that goes down to the depths of their being and that cannot be eradicated without tearing up the roots of personality.... Our entire nature cries out for the living God.

The Psalmist exclaimed long ago, "My heart and my flesh cry out for the living God." And that cry is repeated by every one of us at some time or another in our lives. It is not that part of us desires him; we desire him with every faculty of our being. It is not that our heart desires God while conscience can go without him; it is not that our conscience demands the voice of authority while we can think entirely as we please. The nature of this hunger for God takes in its scope heart and mind and will.

Nor is the hunger for God limited to any particular race or creed or sect. Paul has truly said, "God hath made of one blood all the nations of the earth and determined the times before appointed and the bounds of their habitation, if haply they might feel after him." And in a lofty appeal, the prophet Isaiah utters the voice of God: "If with all your hearts ye truly seek me, ye shall ever surely find me."

We believe and have taught from the beginning that in true religion God takes the initiative. He creates us with hunger for him, and then makes adequate provision to satisfy that hunger. Before we ever knew we needed him, he wanted us for himself. He still does. And he surrounds us with every inducement to come to him. When we do turn to him we feel we have been persuaded to surrender to his will. All true followers of the Lord Jesus say with the apostle of old, "By the grace of God I am what I am." Anyone who thinks through his Christian vocation knows he is not expressing the whole truth when he says that on a certain date "he took up church work." The facts are that above and beyond our own choice is the redemptive love of God, which provided the way in which we are called to work. Our own choice was a factor but the gospel of Christ was already there for us to choose. It was no creation of ours. God took the initiative. He prepared the way. All we have done is to turn to him and by his grace accept that way. No sooner do we become conscious of ourselves than we are conscious of the hand of the Master all about us.

If God loves his children, we must assume that he has loved them from the very beginning, and not that he permitted the race to begin and grow for a long period of years before he turned his kindly countenance upon it and reached down his arms to take it into a loving embrace. God revealed himself long before the first child of Israel was born. Nay, we must go even further and say that God was in readiness to reveal himself before any son of man was born. We read that the heavens declare the glory of God and the firmament showeth his handiwork. Man discovered this fact. As he contemplated it he was lost in wonder and praise. But he only discovered the fact. It existed long before he was born, and shows God's evident purpose in revealing himself to man. He left his mark on the rocks in the hills, on the stars in the heavens, on the waters of the deep, all for the purpose of making himself known to man.

"We love him because he first loved us." Our faith is not fashioned by human minds but rests upon and revolves around the story of definite acts done by God for our salvation. The disciple of Christ stands forth not simply to proclaim what he feels but to tell the world that which God has done. The Christian faith is inexorably opposed to the notion of self-redemption. It is the movement of God toward us to which we respond. The initiative lies with him. We initiate nothing.

George Fox, a devout and able man and an early

Quaker, bears a testimony which is of interest
at this point:

Now the Lord God opened to me by his invisible power "that
every man was enlightened by the divine light of Christ"; and
I saw it shine through all; and that they that believed in
it came out of condemnation to the light of life, and
became the children of it; but they that hated it, and did
not believe in it, were condemned by it, though they made
a profession of Christ. This I saw in the pure openings of
the light, without the help of any man; neither did I then
know where to find it in the scriptures, though afterwards,
searching the scriptures, I found it. For I saw, in that light
and spirit which was before the scriptures were given forth,
and which led the holy men of God to give them forth,
that all must come to that spirit if they would know God,
or Christ, or the scriptures aright, which they that gave them
forth were led and taught by.—*Authority and the Light Within*,
page 71.

The way in which God takes the initiative is
clearly seen in the story of the prophets of Israel
and the accounts they themselves give of their
commissions. During the three hundred years from
Amos to Malachi there was a continuous succession
of prophets whose writings are preserved to us.
Let us listen to some typical utterances:

I was no prophet, neither was I a prophet's son; but I was
an herdsman, and a dresser of sycamore trees: and the Lord
took me from the following the flock, and the Lord said
unto me, Go, prophesy unto my people Israel. Now therefore
hear the word of the Lord. . . .

But I truly am full of power by the spirit of the Lord,
and of judgment, and of might, to declare unto Jacob his
transgression, and to Israel his sin. . . .

Mine heart within me is broken, all my bones shake; I am
like a drunken man, and like a man whom wine hath
overcome; because of the Lord, and because of his holy

words....Is not my word like as fire? saith the Lord; and like a hammer that breaketh the rock in pieces?

Such passages recur constantly. The prophets, then, because they are conscious of being thus even violently dealt with and possessed, claim to utter with supreme authority a word or message from God to man. The content of this message is, on the whole, quite clear in its final outcome. It is a message which proclaims God as intensely personal and moral, as the one and only God, the absolute Creator and Sustainer and Judge of all that is almighty in the sense that no other god or external power exists to restrain him.

It proclaims him in unmistakable terms for a practical purpose—not, that is, with a view to the satisfaction of metaphysical inquiries but for the sole purpose of making his people understand that there is no manner of fellowship with him possible except by conformity to his character; that is, by goodness, social and individual, by "doing justly, and loving mercy, and walking humbly with God."

FAITH

No matter from which angle we approach in the task of understanding Jesus, the outstanding significance of his faith soon becomes apparent. It is the key to his greatness. We see at once that Jesus' faith is much more than a plank in a creedal platform. Jesus gave little time to specific formulation of doctrinal teaching. Nor is the faith of Jesus limited to visible things. On the contrary, some invisible things were more real to the Master because of his faith than the tangible things with which he was surrounded. Such was the keenness of his insight that he saw that the only hope of permanence lies in beauty and truth and goodness. He readily recognized that all else fades or is swept away before the onrush of time and expanding experience. So the invisible good which had not yet been achieved was to him more sure and abiding than the visible evil which surrounded him on all sides.

To Jesus, the fact that God is, and that God loves, guarantees the ultimate triumph of righteousness, so that men will endure the temptations of riches. This is much more than faith in facts. It is faith in a person. And since faith is the response of the soul of Jesus, it is a vital aspect of all that he did and taught.

The faith of Jesus was more than belief. As James

said: "The devils believe and tremble." The word *belief* is not sufficiently vital to express the purposeful attitude of Jesus. To the Master, God was so great a Father that the attribution of the word *Father* to him has given that word added significance ever since. The faith of Jesus was an intimate fellowship with his Father, resulting in his continuing identification with the divine purpose. His faith was the response of his life to the divine fatherhood. It was a way of living rather than just a way of thinking. The whole life of the Master is explicable from the viewpoint of this living faith. It explains, for example, the fundamental harmony of the teaching and actions of Jesus throughout the course of his ministry.

Moreover, the faith of the Master was more than belief in faith. Some people believe in the efficacy of faith without having faith themselves. But to Jesus, faith in God was a way of living in affectionate response to the winning and comprehensive love of his Father. To him, faith was like a true marriage. It demanded letting himself go, forgetting doubts and hesitations, and venturing his life on affection and confidence. The vindication of such an adventure lies in experience, and the faith of the Master was abundantly vindicated in the quality of his living which resulted therefrom.

Most of us come to understand the teachings of Jesus gradually in one of two general ways: Either we come to know him and then study his teachings, or vice versa. We do not use either of these methods exclusively, but sometimes the one method predominates over the other.

To some people Jesus first appeals as a most wonderful friend, satisfying their best desires and their most eager longings for spiritual communion. His friendship and the winsomeness of his personality attract them before they begin to analyze the reason for his appeal. Then, later, in an endeavor to find the secret of his power, such people consider his faith, or his love, or his fearlessness. Yet each phase of his life and teaching has in it something of his whole personality—something of his sympathy, something of his wide range of belief, of his unfaltering courage and loyalty, of his hunger for the souls of men, of his never failing communion with God. When we seek to discover the sources of his power, some of these aspects of his personality fall into the background, but whatever may be in the foreground for the time is meaningless unless the man Jesus stands behind and explains and gives cohesion and unity through the fact of his well-rounded life.

This is quite similar to the process of friendship. Our hearts go out to some people before we know them. Such persons make a certain winning appeal which defies analysis and which we sense as more significant than the sum of their various qualities. As we get to know them more, we probe beneath the surface of their friendship to find and label the sources of their attractiveness, but even though we might talk about the tact and self-control and the intelligence and courtesy of these friends, we know that in each case the whole man is shining through that part of him which we have labeled. It is not merely intelligence that we admire and love, but his intelligence; not merely courtesy, but the intelligent courtesy which he manifests.

So it is with Jesus. Some people get to know him before they know of the sources of his strength; forever afterward, even though they may talk about the faith or courage or loyalty of the Master, their love is for him who shines through these attributes and speaks peace to their souls, and not just for faith or courage or loyalty as abstract qualities.

We have noticed the same process at work in the lives of young immigrants who have been in the United States a short time but are nevertheless won by the idealism of American institutions. They admire the national characteristics. They are proud of their residence in America and of their determination to become naturalized. Then some particular incident arises, and in effect they say: "This is what an American would do." And through their doing of that one thing shines all that citizenship means to them.

In this way we can learn of the faith of Jesus. It is part of his life. It is not a small and separate thing to be explained in logical terms and to be examined apart from the other manifestations of his goodness. The whole life of the Master is an expression of his faith. All his teaching is the teaching of a supremely faithful Son. Every act is centered in faith. To many of us the way to understand the faith of Jesus is to get to know Jesus first, to bask in the totality of his friendship, and then to seek the faithful element in all that he means to us.

● ● ●

We are the inheritors of a most wonderful spiritual tradition—an inheritance that not only gives meaning to the past but offers guidance for the future. We must examine briefly this tradition and bear in mind while we do so that it does not stand alone; it is environed in a living process which encompasses the deeds of all men of all time and the behavior of every element in existence.

What is the faith of the church? What was "once delivered unto the saints"? Let us bear in mind that it is a "faith," not a system of morals, nor a code of ethics, nor a panacea for the ills of the world. This faith is an assumption of the truth and an enlightenment based upon a revelation of that truth. It is not a philosophy of existence but an insight into the life of God. It is not illumined by reason or logic, but it corrects, sanctifies, and hallows these wholly human activities. It is not a rigid system of thought or a moral equation like a scientific formula. It is a clue to the meaning of the whole. It is not blind trust in an unimaginable mystery. It is an inward light which sheds its radiance on the pathway before us. It is not an uprush from the dark unfathomed caverns of the human mind, nor the rationalization of a "mysterium tremendum" which some say lies behind the visible world. It is a gift reaching downward from the "Father of Lights." "The Faith" (and we use the capital "F") is not a key idea leading to enlightened thought. It is something enkindled in man, and is the urge to righteous action. Santayana has described faith as an "invincible surmise," and the Book of Mormon informs us that it is "wrought" in the soul by the Spirit of God.

The faith of the church is best understood as we direct our minds toward God. When we think only of each other, then that faith wavers and our sight grows dim, and the sense of direction uncertain. The gospel does not originate in the minds of men, nor in their needs. It originates in the nature of God. It is a disclosure of the truth. On this basis alone it urges its claim to meet human needs.

There exists no expert wise enough or brave enough to diagnose the ills of the world, let alone rash enough to prescribe a remedy for them. In the midst of Paradise, we are told, there is a tree, the leaves of which are "for the healing of the nations." This delightful parable represents the fact that the truth alone will make men free.

Pilate asked the question, "What shall I do with Jesus, which is called Christ?" This question is always asked by those whose minds are directed only outward and never upward. For the Christian faith it is an irrelevant question. It is not, "What shall I do with Jesus, which is called Christ?" but "What will Christ do with me?" Our faith is based on a true disclosure of the nature of God in Christ. Whatever it bestows on life or thought, ethics or morals, politics or economics springs from the fact that it is true. The primary question is not even "Will it work?" The primary question is, "Is it true?" It claims to be the Spirit of the Whole revealed to those whom God wills. It does not abolish or set aside what men know about matter, life, and mind but transforms such knowledge in its own light.

Those to whom Jesus came had some knowledge of

God and of his law. This knowledge Jesus extended and completed. He taught no pharisaical code; even his teaching was not, as far as we know, presented in systematic form, but he did claim to be the Light and Life of the world. In him could all life be illumined and all human activity reoriented. No system of reasoning could have revealed him to be this. The fundamental truths stemming from the gospel are apprehended only as a result of a new birth of man's entire being brought about by the action of God within the soul.

Faith always outruns reason. Faith is vindicated in life, and life is always in advance of thought. This does not mean that faith is irrational. It means, simply, that faith is of the whole man, an illumination which is itself a divine gift, and in the light of which man is given direction and rational grounds for his reason. There is no legitimate field of human life or thought into which the faithful Christian may not safely and freely and intelligently go, and therein find confirmation of his faith.

What does this amount to? We are to be persuaded by the Spirit of the truth that "God is in Christ, reconciling the world unto himself." The persuasion is first upward to God. Second, and only second, it is outward toward men. As the disclosure of God in Christ draws men upward, so will it bring them together. Any attempt to begin at the other end, with the mistakes and ills of the world, calling on Divinity simply to heal these, will end in failure, or at best in but partial success. A complete healing of the nations begins in a new man and ends in a new heaven and a new earth, and the new man is born from above as he cooperates freely and willingly with God.

Faith must justify itself. It does this in the lives of

those who trust in God. Such justification of faith in life issues in a complete and comprehensive soul-satisfying system of thought which is unique. The acceptance in faith of this gospel—namely, that God was in Christ—accords with procedures in the fields of art and science.

The basic assumptions of art seem to be the unity of life, the universality of beauty, and the sheer inevitability of artistic form. Similarly, the scientist accepts the universal reign of law as a dogma even before he knows what that law is in its entirety. This is illustrated in the fact that Albert Einstein unsuccessfully searched for a "unified field theory" which would completely explain the structure and nature of matter.

This does not prevent others from holding the conviction that there was and is such a theory. Now comes the news that Professor Eisenberg feels that he may have succeeded, although years of further research will be necessary to determine if he has done so or not. So the search goes on, conditioned and sustained in faith.

Similarly, the faith of the church is expressed in the ever growing quest for truth and the deepening convictions of her people as these are sustained by worship—worship based on the belief that God is, and is a "rewarder of those who diligently seek him." So without faith it is impossible to please him. In describing this approach to reality—the gospel approach—we are describing a procedure which is productive of truth and beauty everywhere.

The gospel deals with human relationships, but only in a secondary sense. Primarily, the gospel is a declaration of the nature and mind of God, and is concerned first to secure the proper relationship of man to his

Maker. Human relationships not founded on this primary consideration are based on shifting sands and thus are insecure.

The revelation of God in Christ comes first—and out of this issues a covenanted relation between man and God. Charity is a fruitage of this revelation and can grow in man from no other source.

This is another way of stating the great commandment, "Thou shalt love the Lord thy God with all thy heart, might, mind and strength, and thy neighbor as thyself."

● ● ●

According to John, the divine Word bodied forth the universe. He is seen in the rising of the sun in the morning as well as in the rising of God's Son from the dead. All things are of him (the Word). The eternal Word of God, the breath of God's lips, the underlying rationale of all things was made flesh, so that we might rightly conceive the nature of God.

Faith in God, rightly conceived, will issue eventually in a transformed society, and conviction that such a society will inevitably appear sustains the faithful in their sacrificial endeavors. They not only thus anticipate history but actually participate in framing it. But faith in the God of our Lord Jesus Christ is ever and always the ground of such endeavor. We may well inquire now as to the nature of Christ's revelation of God.

Jesus came to those who had already gained a unique conception of the Divine. The Jews of his day regarded the Old Testament and their own history much as we regard the history of our own nation. We ourselves are

76

the latest phase of that history; they were of theirs. They did not regard their background as we might think of the history of the Chinese, from a critical outside point of view. The Jews of Jesus' day had with them a conviction of the nature of God based on a sympathetic view of the Old Testament and their own history to its latest phase. This Jesus took for granted and indeed was himself schooled in this point of view, a point of view which reflected the fact that the Old Testament was a living thing, and that in some sense it was incomplete since a revival of the ancient prophetic fire was hoped for and looked for. There are several aspects of this living faith which Jesus enlarged and completed which we must note.

First, God is One, and he is holy and utterly righteous. This conviction was a product of history interpreted by the prophets. In earlier times, it seems, Yahweh was the God of Israel much as Chemosh was the god of Moab. Even Joshua admonishes his people to put away "the gods," whom he appears to take for granted.

While Israel's God is a jealous God, according to the Decalogue, and others are not to be served or seriously regarded, it is not until after the Exile that the conviction is secured that there is no other God in existence. The people went into Babylon uncertain on this point. Only those who believed the prophets had the stamina and stability to return and rebuild Jerusalem. So the captivity bore fruit, religiously, in that it left to Israel the conviction, "I am the Lord . . . there is no God beside me." This one God was righteous. In all the earth he judged and "did right." He was consistent and utterly true to himself, and thus holy.

Rudolf Otto has, in recent years, made it clear that to

primitive peoples especially there is a spirit of dreadful mystery in the universe and this occasions their awe and worship. The Hebrew people came gradually to associate this spirit with the majesty of the "law of the Lord," which converts "the soul." So, for them, conscience was indeed a "stern daughter of the voice of God," and his unity and absolute purpose was holy and righteous.

Second, God is personal and living. There are some lofty ideas about ultimate reality in the philosophy of Plato and his pupil, Aristotle. To them God is remote and seemingly impervious to human fortune. He is high and exalted and he inhabits eternity, but he is primarily an object of intellectual contemplation. For the philosophers, God is not a being to be loved and obeyed, one who wants and desires the obedience of men. In the Far East, the doctrine of Nirvana prevailed and God was thought of in terms of a presence pervading all, like a vast sea, with no one above and beyond controlling it. But to Israel, God was a living God, who created all things and who created man, his creature, and who, furthermore, made man in his own image and after his own likeness. Israel did not reach this conclusion either by philosophy or by contemplation. It was a conviction born in them by the prophets who interpreted and sometimes guided their history. It originated in a divine utterance—"Thus saith the Lord."

Those who wrote the Old Testament were concerned with the doings of men only incidentally. Primarily, they were concerned about the doings of God, what he purposed and what he wanted. In a sense the Old Testament is a commentary on the history, the judgments, and the misfortunes of God who, in Isaiah's tremendous phrase, was "made . . . to serve with thy sins," and who was eventually to "bear the sin of many." When the nation became involved in the struggles between great empires, and their small tribal concerns seemed almost incidental, then it was that prophecy developed into apocalypse and vast movements were seen on the background of long periods of time. This was a justification and an extension of the unity and power of God who, despite the tremendous issues involved, still, in the end, asserted his complete control of the historical process. Even if these contending powers all but destroyed Israel, always there would remain an indestructible "remnant."

God is Creator, he is holy, but he is also like a Father. This idea came in Israel's history and never quite appears to be dominant. Moses asked for the preservation of Israel so that God could vindicate himself, not because he might love them. But gradually it came to be a certainty that along with his other attributes, while perhaps subordinate to them, God loved Israel.

The Lord is merciful and gracious, slow to anger, and plenteous in mercy. He will not always chide; neither will he keep his anger for ever. He hath not dealt with us after the manner of our sins, nor rewarded us according to our iniquities. For as the heaven is high above the earth, so great is his mercy toward them that fear him. As far as the east is from the west, so far hath he removed our transgressions from us. Like as a father pitieth his children, so the Lord pitieth them that fear him. For he knoweth our frame; he remembereth that we are dust.—Psalm 103:8-14.

God is king as well as judge. Thus comes the idea of the kingdom. He had called Abraham out of Ur and given to him a land of promise. Israel was "chosen." Israel's people were a special people. Under David and Solomon the kingdom had been glorious. Now, in Jesus' day, Israel was in bondage to Rome. The Jews looked for deliverance, it is true, but much more than deliverance. They looked for God's specially anointed One to restore to them the ancient glories of the kingdom of David.

In this they were almost certainly completely self-centered. The highest reaches of prophetic insight indicated that their choosing was based on God's indiscriminate and impartial love for all men, and that Israel was chosen to be used by God, not to be served but to serve. It was left to Jesus to make this crystal clear; the common man never grasped it.

Indeed, even after the death and resurrection of our Lord, his apostles asked if this now was the time he would restore the kingdom of Israel. So the common man of Jesus' day was "slow of heart" to believe all that the prophets had spoken. While he was convinced that the Israelites were called out and were a "chosen people," the common man never grasped fully the purpose of their calling.

They did not realize wholly the nature of that God who had so wonderfully blessed them, and who was now ready to speak to them by his Son, whom he has appointed heir to all things, by whom also he made the worlds.

* * *

Faith in God is the key that unlocks the mysteries of the divine kingdom. "The time has come, when according to men's faith shall it be done unto them" (Doctrine and Covenants). Faith is a *way of knowledge* just as surely as logic or reason. Faith is not the antithesis of reason. It is not an enemy of logic. Faith is a means whereby certain timeless and eternal truths are committed to us. These eternal and timeless truths, moreover, can be communicated to us in no other way.

Faith reveals certain facts about the nature of the world, of man, and of God which can never be discovered by scientific, logical, or rationalistic methods. When these facts, facts disclosed by the process of revelation, are accepted and laid alongside the facts which are discovered by logic and science, they alter the whole meaning of the structure of the universe for us. Knowledge of these facts revealed by faith does not alter or abrogate knowledge discovered in the sciences. Knowledge of them, however, does modify the value of these other disciplines. The world view which is based on revelation may include in its compass all that men have discovered to be the truth everywhere. Revelation is the catalysis; the truths distilled from it change the value of every other human discovery, while they themselves remain unchanged and unchanging.

The scientist and the logician, each in his field of inquiry, exercise a certain quality of faith. The scientist trusts in the constancy and the intelligibility of nature and, with the logician, trusts implicitly that the deliverance of his senses will lead him to truth. He who hopes to arrive at truth must believe in the essential rationality of his own mind. In all of this, of course, he may be mistaken. But this possibility of mistake does not rob him of the spirit of action which launches him into his discipline. Faith is the spirit of action. No one can assist in the work of science or philosophy except he be humble and full of charity (sympathetic imagination), with his eye single to the glory of God (the intelligence displayed in the behavior of the outer world).

The faith of the scientist and the philosopher has nature as its partner, including human nature. Nature and human nature are fit subjects for hardheaded analysis. Faith in God has revelation as its copartner. Faith is actualized in true Christianity and rests in the divine self-disclosure shown forth in certain acts in history, the validity of which is attested by the divine Spirit. The divine Spirit is given in this peculiar measure to those who love God, who purify themselves before him, and who seek to know his purpose so that they can commit themselves to it.

Faith in God demands the consecration of the whole personality of man. Other disciplines do not. They require only that part of a man or that area of his faculties which is appropriate to their particular disciplines. As an illustration of this we have only to remember that some scientists have been traitors to their own country. It seems that disciplines outside of the divine kingdom do not require the dedication of the whole man as a necessary condition of success. But faith in God does require the whole man—body, mind, and spirit.

To know God involves faith, revelation, *and reason.* Revelation does not seem ever to be in the form of utter and complete proof. It is sustained by faith, critically appreciated by reason, and is a continuous process in the lives of the committed.

Our heavenly Father never overrides our intelligence making us to believe or know what our humanity cannot encompass. If, for instance, there were factual proof of the Incarnation, and such evidence were complete, it would *compel* belief. It would mean intellectual assent rather than discipleship.

Mental submission does not necessarily lead to commitment in faith. The Doctrine and Covenants exhibits the divine Spirit as saying, "Come, let us reason together." Faith in the process of revelation leads always to the dialectic. And the dialectical process is nothing unless it satisfies our reason. If faith could be proved by philosophy, it would lose every vestige of its religious quality. But faith develops a philosophy of its own from the "hidden wisdom" in the keeping of Divinity. Trust is the essence of faith. Faith is the spirit of adventurous activity, and repentance, or adjustment toward the deliverances of the process of revelation, is the activity itself. Faith is related to action. Belief has to do with mental conquest.

Where faith violates reason it loses all moral claim to trust and loyalty. Faith is a starting point, not a conclusion. And, broadly speaking, the primary assumptions of faith in God are the end for which philosophy strives.

Reason serves faith by providing a means of communication.

But sanctify the Lord God in your hearts; and be ready always to give an answer in meekness and fear to every man that asketh of you a reason for the hope that is in you: having a good conscience.— I Peter 3:15, 16.

Reason serves faith by providing a method of relating faith to life. Everyone ought to do his duty. But there is a prior demand to this. He ought to find out what his duty really is. This he can do only by applying the best faculty of mind he has to every concrete situation.

Reason serves faith by criticizing and testing faith against and with the canons of logic and broad human experience. Long ago Socrates said that the unexamined life is not worth living (Apology 38). Paul was in line then with the best philosophic tradition when he said, "So let a man examine himself" (I Corinthians 11:28). "Examine yourselves, whether ye be in the faith; prove your own selves" (II Corinthians 13:5).

Reason performs another service to faith. Reason correlates (not necessarily verifies) the deliverances of the scientific process and by analogy relates them harmoniously to the world view which is implicit in revelation. Paul does this when justifying belief in the resurrection from the dead, and Christ used nature and the doings of men to reveal and illustrate the nature of his Father and his Father's kingdom. We reason from what we discover in nature and the history of man and thereby enlarge and enrich our faith in God.

Karl Barth has the idea that natural theology leads to idols and metaphysical vagaries. He says that God is not only unprovable and unsearchable but also inconceivable. From an exclusive metaphysical point of view he may be right. But reason can and must analyze the facts of experience. Those who have had experience with God have found their minds enlightened and their faculties quickened. Into their hands are placed facts of which the sciences are totally ignorant. Sir Arthur Eddington has said, "Something unknown is doing we do not know what."

The scientists experience process but know nothing of purpose which initiates, guides, and fulfills the process. It is in the realm of purpose that we must seek the revelation of Divinity. Only God can tell us who he is. Only God can tell us what he will do. Only God can tell us what he wants us to do. Faith in these propositions is based upon the testimony of the Scriptures and a knowledge of history. Faith in these propositions will lead to that disciplined search at the end of which there is always the divine self-disclosure to each and every man who undertakes it. "For he that cometh to God must first believe that he is." Faith in God leads to a knowledge of his purpose and such knowledge is not inconsistent with knowledge gained from every avenue of endeavor to which man has put mind.

JESUS

The Christian religion is centered in certain historical facts. It is not primarily a series of ideas, nor is it first a philosophy of life. It is based on what happened, not upon some myth which might please the fancy. It is basically the story of what God has done for man, and of his revelation of himself in the course of time.

If there is a God, and careful thought leads us to suppose there is, and if he is truly person—if God is a "Thou"—then he must reveal himself. Self-revelation is the primary characteristic of persons. A being incapable of making himself known would be less than fully personal. The highest manifestation of the being of God must of necessity be in the life of personality. His power may be shown forth in the mighty storm. Space may tell he is great. The intense fertility of the insects indicates he is incessantly creative. Nature may tell us of aspects of his character which render us spellbound and keep us held in fascinated awe. But if God himself is to show us who and what he is, he must appear in a personal way to his creatures.

The good news which constitutes the heart of the gospel is that such a personal revelation actually took place at a certain time, and in a definite location, and on the historical plane known to all of us. This is the one factor which binds together Christians of all ages.

Jesus came at the climax of a long series of prophetic

episodes in Israel's history which were designed to prepare people for his advent. The Hebrew people had a genius for religion and felt that even though God had created all men, he had chosen them to be the vehicle of a special manifestation of the Divine. The promise to the fathers was twofold. First, "In thee and thy seed shall all nations of the earth be blessed"; and second, as a means of implementing the promise, "This land will I give thee for an everlasting possession."

At first the national consciousness engendered by these peoples was extremely narrow and selfish. Frequently Israel wandered after other gods, and just as frequently they were reclaimed by the heroic and farsighted ministry of the prophets. Always the prophets sought to keep before the people the vision of their national destiny. And by the time Jesus appeared, after the Jews had passed through many stern disciplines, their spiritual perception was leavened by a sense of universality and expanding moral responsibility.

Even a cursory view of the Old Testament will convince us that the thought of the prophets is directed again and again to the glorious days which lie ahead—days when all wrong shall be made right. And Israel, the nation, should come into its own under the leadership of the coming Messiah-King.

The Jews looked backward to the time of Abraham as the day when they were specifically chosen for their distinctive service. Paul designates the promises to Abraham as evidence of the foreordination of Jesus. Moses looked for the coming of a prophet like him, yet greater than he. But it is Isaiah, more than all, who foretells in language of sheer beauty of the coming of the "child of hope, the Wonderful, the Counsellor, the Mighty God, the Everlasting Father, the Prince of Peace" who, by the "zeal of the Lord of Hosts, would be established upon the throne of David and rule in judgment and with justice for evermore"; and even though he should be thus established would nevertheless be a "man of sorrows and acquainted with grief," "bruised for our iniquities, wounded for our transgressions, with the chastisement of our peace upon him."

The quality of the leadership to be offered by this Messiah was clearly designated in the words, "I, the Lord, have called thee in righteousness and will give thee . . . for a covenant of the people, for a light to the Gentiles; to open the blind eyes, to bring out prisoners from the prison, and them that sit in darkness out of the prison-house." Jesus was to quote these passages when he first began his ministry.

The two thousand years over which these prophetic utterances had been made found the Israelites growing from a small nomadic family to a mighty people with dominion from Egypt to the Euphrates. During all this time they had been torn with internal dissension, divided, scattered, regathered, liberated, and reconquered. These chosen people were harried and subdued by their neighbors and at times they questioned the promises. But under the inspired leadership of the prophets they came gradually to realize that divine favor was predicated solely upon righteousness. The prophets always denounced wickedness, yet they held out hope of eventual deliverance upon conditions of righteousness.

By the time the Jews returned from the Babylonish captivity, it seems they had learned well the lesson of the holiness of God, and so they went to the other extreme. They multiplied ceremonial rites and clouded men's approach to the Eternal; and their religion became a burden.

Always since his day the people had loved David and hoped that eventually a descendant of his would sit on his throne and avenge them of their wrongs. In the second century before Christ, the Greek, Antiochus Epiphanes, persecuted the Hebrew people and they revolted under Judas Maccabees; but they were soon to be subjected again by Rome. So the Jews began to hope, then, that the Divine would manifest his power through the Messiah to the overthrow of the Roman yoke, the vindication of the righteous, and the destruction of the wicked. And so it was a day of great expectation when John the Baptist came on the scene. He was the last of the great prophets. In him the spirit of prophecy was gloriously revived, and he was a contemporary of the Master. He began his preparatory ministry in the fifteenth year of Tiberius—or about A.D. 27.

When John the Baptist appeared, not the oldest man in Palestine could remember having spoken even in his earliest childhood with any man who had seen a prophet. In these circumstances, the appearance of a new prophet was an occurrence of the first magnitude, more significant than war or revolution.

By any standard, John was a very remarkable man. He became the center of a great religious revival, and yet he was humble enough to recognize he was a forerunner, as nothing in comparison to his successor. He came, preaching the coming of the kingdom for which all Israel was looking. He hoped to arouse his people to look forward to a new day of faith. To the ceremony of baptism he gave added significance by telling of one who would come after him, but who in reality was preferred before him, who would baptize not only with water but with fire and with the Holy Ghost.

● ● ●

The term "Jesus Christ" designates a historical person who lived in Palestine during the reigns of the Roman emperors Augustus and Tiberius, but it also designates one who has been the object of Christian faith and worship for almost twenty centuries. These two designations may be distinguished, indeed they must be; but they cannot be separated. For almost everything we know about the historical person comes from the reports of those who addressed faith and worship to Him. The portraits of Jesus in the Gospels are the testimony of "faith to faith."—*Encyclopaedia Britannica.*

We see One who was born by no activity of human will, but only by the acquiescence of the Virgin-Mother in the divine Will; who called men to such a dependence on and fellowship with God as had never been conceived, yet lived always as one who Himself experienced what He taught; who died at the hands of those He called to share His blessedness, and in the very hour of His anguish prayed for their forgiveness; who rose bodily from the grave, and closed his appearances to His disciples by the enacted parable of His Ascension from the mountain whereon they stood till He was enveloped in the cloud of the divine glory.—William Temple

There are but few references to Jesus in history outside the four gospels. But even though few in number they are fairly convincing as proof that Jesus actually lived.

Tacitus, a well known historian writing about A.D. 111, does not mention Jesus very favorably. He held that the Christian religion was a pernicious superstition, although he believed Christians to be innocent of the charges which led to their persecution by Nero. The Annals of Tacitus contains one of the earliest witnesses to the Crucifixion in non-Christian literature.

Seutonius was secretary to the Emperor Hadrian and a contemporary of Tacitus. He writes in his *Life of*

Claudius, "Since the Jews continually made disturbances at the instigation of Christ, he (i.e. Claudius) expelled them from Rome."

Pliny the Younger, who was governor of Bythinia, asked the emperor Trajan whether Christians should be persecuted simply because of their name. He had executed some of them, but investigation had revealed their generally good character, and he writes for advice from the Emperor, hinting that tolerance might be in order. This letter was written about A.D. 112.

Lucien, a satirist, wrote of Jesus as a master who persuaded a group of followers that they were brothers and would live forever.

Josephus, the Jewish historian, mentions the condemnation of "James, the brother of Jesus, the so-called Messiah."

No reputable historian ever committed himself to any theory which denies that Jesus was a Jew of the first century. But there are those who tell us that Jesus is a myth, created out of men's imagination. But such ask us to believe in a literary miracle far more stupendous than those recorded in the gospels. Shakespeare embodied for us in some of his characters the propensities which all seem to share in some degree. Thus Othello embodies jealousy, Skylock embodies greed, and so forth. But what kind of mind would it take to invent the love and the life and the light that dwells in Jesus? Certainly such an invention or myth would require a character equal to that it imagines.

Those who would have us believe that the story of Jesus is wholly the product of some human imagination fail to appreciate the principle that only he who is great can appreciate greatness in others. No man is spiritually alert enough to paint such a picture as the Gospels present unless he had an actual model before him. The experience of men down through the ages is that Jesus is nobler, kindlier, stronger, and more compassionate than any man or any set of men. The testimony of sixty generations is that Jesus is not the product of human imagination but the result of divine disclosure. At its best, human imagination, scanning the past and reaching into the future, has never yet scaled the heights nor plumbed the depths of the love, the life, and the light revealed in Jesus Christ. The great testimony to the reality of Jesus, to his historicity, lies in the fact that he still lives in the hearts of men. If one may say so, we are not utterly dependent upon the New Testament for evidence that Christ lived on the earth and still lives. The whole history of the church necessitates him.

The true Christian reads the accounts of the Master's life in order to share the experience of those who walked and talked with him while he was here on earth. Roman historians, Jewish unbelievers, as well as the Christian apologists all join to bear testimony to the historicity of Jesus Christ.

As scholars have probed into the background of the literature of the New Testament, the majority of them have agreed with Harnack who was the outstanding scholar of patristic literature of the last generation. He wrote in 1897 his "Chronology of Ancient Christian Literature" in which he said:

There was a time, and the general public is still at that date, when it was considered necessary to hold the most ancient Christian literature, including the New Testament, as a tissue of deception and falsehood. That time has now passed. For science it was an episode in which she learned much, and after which she has much to forget. The results of my investigations go in a reactionary sense far beyond what one might call the moderate position in the criticism of today. The most ancient literature of the Church is, on all chief points and in the majority of details, veracious and worthy of belief from the point of view of literary history.

When this writing first appeared it created a sensation as coming from one who had shared the more destructive opinions, and who still in his beliefs about Christ remained far removed from orthodoxy.

There is a simplicity and straightforward honesty about the gospel narratives which stamp them with the seal of authenticity. The writers make no endeavor to embellish the facts. They make no obvious comment. After a lapse of years the writers sensed in Jesus a personality so supreme that in painting his picture for friends they would not mar that picture by putting themselves, by comments, into the remote background. Jesus was still so vivid to them that they sought only to tell his story. They were convinced that in so writing, the radiance of the Master's personality would shine through their work and win others to him as they themselves had been won.

Would you learn of the Master? Would you sit at his feet? If you would, the opportunity is extended to you in the writings of the New Testament. These writings are humanity's most treasured literary possession. Let us not neglect them, lest in the day of judgment it be said of us that we neglected so great salvation.

● ● ●

Of the painting, "The Magnificent Madonna" by Botticelli, William Temple says:

. . . There are not so many figures of outstanding beauty but the picture is a single whole; one may study it point by point and appreciate it the better in consequence; but its impression is single and its meaning is one and indivisible.

We may notice [in the picture] that the child is reading his mother's song, moving his finger along the words; he has reached the word "humilitatem," and pausing there, has thrown back his head to look up in her face, as though to say "Ah! That was it: we know about that"; and she leans over him: and is quite unconscious that from behind her the angels are lowering a crown upon her head.... Nothing else exists but the Divine humility, and the crown which quite unconsciously it wears.... If anybody wants to know what the greatest picture in the world is like, he must go to Florence and look at it....

As soon as he could utter words, Jesus was taught the "Shema," which was the Jewish confession of faith. While at home, young Jesus spoke Aramaic although he must have learned Greek also, because on several occasions he spoke to the Gentiles without an interpreter. His education was furthered by frequent visits made to Jerusalem, where the Passover was celebrated and where he learned some of the facts of his country's past history. From the hilltop near his home he could see the famous plain of Esdraelon upon which in imagination he could live again the famous battles of his country's history. Right through his village ran the highway from Syria to Egypt, where the legions of Rome marched. Jesus watched men and listened intently to their conversation. "Here were wonderful opportunities for observation and conversation such as would enrich his mind and broaden his understanding, for Jesus as a boy watched men more closely than they guessed: on whose ears words fell, not as old coinages but as new minting, with the marks of thought still rough and bright upon them— indexes to the speaker."

We do not know very much about the early life of Jesus. People who love him feel very keenly the absence from the Gospels of a more detailed account of his early life. But if we try to reconstruct that early life we must have recourse to the parables. Matthew tells us a little when he recounts the flight into Egypt, and his purpose was evidently to indicate the fulfillment of prophecy. Luke, the doctor, who took pains to inquire into the origins of Christianity, evidently secured the story of the Temple incident from Mary, the mother of Jesus. For these two brief recitations we must be grateful. But the human interest stories which Jesus himself told later contain a wealth of suggestion. Imagine him coming in from his father's workshop with a tear in his clothes. "Put on another patch, Mother, please," he would have said. But Mary's experience was that one reaches the point, after a while, when patches do not pay. Jesus remembered and years later he discomfited the religious leaders with the remark that new patches on old garments are quite impractical.

Joseph and Mary were not rich, nor were they learned, but they were the kind of people who formed the backbone of the nation. While they avoided extremes, yet they looked forward with intense faith to the coming of Messiah; and when Jesus came to them, they must have watched him with loving care, conscious of the tremendous stewardship which had been invested in them. Mary, his mother, is the most frequently mentioned member of Jesus' family. He had four half-brothers, James, Joseph, Simon, and Judah, and two half-sisters. There is a tradition that soon after the Temple incident, when Jesus arrived at his early teens, Father Joseph died. As was the well-established custom, the eldest son assumed the responsibility of caring for the family, and this of course fell to the lot of Jesus. As a boy he had learned to work in the carpenter shop, for idleness was not a Jewish trait. Every boy had to learn a trade. And so the "Son of man" who had been with his Father on the morn of creation, and whose word had framed the worlds, now found himself at the carpenter's bench with the tools of his trade in his hands.

He who had framed the commandment, "Six days shalt thou labor and do all thy work," now found himself honoring that commandment. Because he did, work has been a sacred thing and all our common tasks illumined with an uncommon glory.

Did he not know then the true meaning of the word *humilitatem*? Is not his utter humility shown forth in his complete subjection of himself to life under human conditions such as we know? He grew from grace to grace; he did not know all things at once. But at every stage of his human development he represents the Divine, as far as God can be revealed at that stage of human development. He was precocious, as evidenced by his conversation with the doctors in the Temple, but the wonder of his life is revealed in the few words which followed his discovery in the temple, "And he went down with them [his parents], and came to Nazareth and was subject unto them: but his mother kept all these sayings in her heart."

The population of modern Nazareth is about twenty-five thousand. Although it was probably much smaller in the days of Jesus, its importance was relatively greater then than now. Galilee had a varied population which was quite typical of the Roman world, while that of the village which sheltered the carpenter's family was an epitome of the province. Everyone knew what was happening, and gatherings of the Nazarenes of an evening around the single copious spring, or in the synagogue each Sabbath, made the village life similar to that of a large family.

There was nothing sumptuous about the houses of the peasant families. The small square brick or stone home of Joseph and Mary probably had a single room with a dirt floor, one door, and, possibly, one narrow window. There the family ate and worked by day and slept by night. The level housetop was a welcome "extra room" reached by an outside stairway. On summer evenings the lower room frequently would be deserted, but even if both rooms were used, solitude was difficult. This may have had its part in the formation of the habit of returning to the hillside for prayer. The boy Jesus had had communion with "the Spirit which pervades all nature and speaks of peace" long before the man was forced into similar retreat.

F. Henry Edwards has written:

So Jesus came to gradual maturity, in a real world among real people. From the typical devout home of his people, and from the time he went to school with boys of his own age and, returning, played in the marketplace, and in the face-to-face contacts with his fellows, he developed the manhood which has moved the world.

And so Jesus "increased in wisdom and stature, and in favor with God and man."

● ● ●

Our Lord did not enter into his public ministry until he was thirty years old. Until that time he worked as a carpenter or a master carpenter and provided the necessary means for the sustenance of his family. Some of the significance of this activity is reflected in the rough-hewn lines of G. A. Studdert-Kennedy:

> I wonder what he charged for chairs
>   at Nazareth
> And did men try to beat him down
> And boast about it in the town,
> "I bought it cheap for half-a-crown
> From that mad Carpenter?"
> And did they promise and not pay,
> Did they break His heart that way,
> My Lord the Carpenter?
> I wonder, did he have bad debts
> And did he know my fears and frets?
> The gospel writers here forget
> To tell about the Carpenter.
> But that's just what I want to know.
> Ah! Christ in Glory, here below
> Men cheat and lie to one another so
> It's hard to be a carpenter!

The fact that our Lord so worked identifies him absolutely and completely with those who do the work of the world. Jesus was no ordinary carpenter. There is no doubt but what a man of his genius did not occupy a subordinate position. While he probably had men working for him, he also worked alongside them. He was held in high favor among men, and this explains partly the ready allegiance they gave him. In his daily work he was an example to others and the master-craftsman himself could expect high quality workmanship from those he employed.

Jesus must have been familiar with every home in Nazareth. In his shop, or sitting by the roadside, fashioning yokes or shaping the handles of the plough, repairing the packsaddles and chests belonging to the journeymen, he found ready fellowship with all who came to him. His quiet and searching questioning laid bare to him the hearts and the motives of men, for "he needed not that any man should testify of man, for he knew what was in man."

In a moment of understanding compassion, he stood and invited the men and women of his day to "Come unto me, all ye that labor and are heavy laden, and I will give you rest. Take my yoke upon you and learn of me, for I am meek and lowly in heart, and ye shall find rest to your souls." He who knew how carefully to fashion the yoke to the neck of the ox knew also how to instruct and discipline men to share his responsibilities.

It is possible that Jesus moved to Capernaum some time before he began his public ministry, where the larger and more diversified life would bring him into contact with many of the men who later followed him—Peter, Andrew, James and John, to mention a few. His work offered wonderful opportunities for friendship. But as F. Henry Edwards has said,

There was other happiness in his work for a man such as he. He was more than a workman. He was a craftsman. With the creative artistry so characteristic of his every endeavor, he found in the making of the simple implements of the day an opportunity for self-expression at once satisfying and useful. Pride of workmanship is a real factor in the lives of real men. Nothing ministers quite so completely to the self-respect of men who love their tasks as the joy of definite and beautiful achievement. The yokes smoothly shaped to the shoulder, the chest strongly and squarely built, the door well hung in its frame, the foundation securely set for the house of his friends; all were *his* in a sense they could never belong to their owners, and it is not difficult to imagine him running his hand with lingering affection along the well-rounded plough handle before passing it to the waiting farmer.

Jesus has still a lot to teach our generation about work. He gave always good measure pressed down, shaken together and running over. He was never slovenly, nor did he skimp his work or watch the sundial. He never asked, "What's in this for me?" but rather, "How can I best meet this need?" America faces today many, many foes, not the least of which is the spirit which seeks to get as much as possible for the least outlay. And why do men work anyway? Work is occasioned by human need, and when one is working to supply that need he is in the service of God. In fact our daily work is our chief means of serving him.

He who created the sun and stars and made the earth looked upon what he had done and pronounced it very good. Thus also did Jesus lavish his best efforts on his smallest work, until he could say of it, "Very good."

You who work, do you draw a line down the middle of your life and say to yourself, "This is secular and this is sacred"? Do you go to work only for the paycheck at the end of the week? If you do, God pity you. It is never enough, is it? The reason you go to work is that someone needs what you produce. If any of you are in the kind of job that doesn't minister to human weal, I suggest you change jobs and that you ask the help of the Master Carpenter in so doing. For is it not true that when you are in the service of your fellowmen you are in the service of your God? The need of your fellowmen is your chief opportunity to serve the Almighty, because whatever you do is registered in you.

You don't go to church to build character. You go to church to see the kind of man you ought to be, and then, feeling the swell and the power and the insight of the Spirit, you are invited to go out and toil in the affairs of

100

the men of business and work. As you toil you feel as you did when you were in his presence. Character is made out there six days a week, as you earn your bread.

Servants, be obedient to them that are your masters according to the flesh, . . . not with eye-service, as men-pleasers, but as the servants of Christ, doing the will of God from the heart; . . . knowing that whatsoever good things any man doeth, the same shall he receive of the Lord.

Whatever you do does something to you; the only thing you ever had is what you do. What a man does is what he has.

Our Lord Jesus Christ, knowing this principle, lavished himself on his work. He who made the stars and the suns, the flowers and the birds to sing his praise now found himself beside a carpenter's bench with the tools of his trade, with the burden of caring for his mother and the half-brothers and sisters. And so—every commandment which our Lord gave to his disciples as touching the kingdom of God has been tested in his own experience.

When he said to us, "Thou shalt seek first the kingdom of God to establish his righteousness," he was talking to all of us. Jesus who said, "All are called according to the gifts of God unto them," labored in a carpenter's shop and knew that therein he had an opportunity of serving.

● ● ●

Baptism received externally is symbolical. The going down into the water and being immersed in it is an acted representation of life through death; the dying to an old life and being buried, and rising again to the new life; but it is more than a symbol. It effects what it symbolizes. It is the transference of a man into a new spiritual sphere. It is baptism "into Christ."—Charles Gore, *Reconstruction*, page 745.

At the beginning of his public ministry Jesus presented himself to John for baptism. In this he identified himself with John's movement and with the sinful people he came to save. It is a mistake to assert, as some do, that John minimized the ceremony of baptism by asserting it is incidental to the baptism of the Holy Ghost and fire, which the One who was coming would bring. Jesus submitted himself to the ceremony to fulfill all righteousness. When baptism by water is omitted righteousness in the completest sense remains unfulfilled.

Now before Jesus came there was already in practice among the Jews the rite of baptism, which was submitted to by those who would become proselytes to Judaism. The water in which they were immersed was supposed to wash away the whole unhallowed and unprofitable past, and they were raised out of it new men into a new world. They felt as though death were behind them and they had been born into a higher realm.

No ceremony could possibly be better adapted to Christ's purpose as an initiatory rite to distinguish those within from those outside the movement he initiated. It was already in use and had acquired meanings and associations which all understood. Christ adopted baptism and made it binding upon all his followers to submit to it.

Sir J. R. Seeley has an interesting interpretation of the visit of Nicodemus to Jesus. In the fourth Gospel there is a story which illustrates in a most striking manner the importance which Christ attached to baptism. A man named Nicodemus, of advanced years and influential position, visited Christ, we are told, in secret, and entered into conversation with him. He began by an explicit avowal of belief in Christ's divine mission. What he would have gone on to say we may conjecture from these two facts—namely, that he believed in Christ and that nevertheless he visited him secretly. It appears that he hoped to comply with Christ's demand of personal homage and submission but to be excused from making a public avowal of it. And when we consider the high position of Nicodemus, it is natural to suppose that he had hoped to receive such a special exemption in consideration of the services he had it in his power to render. He could push the movement among the influential classes; he could cautiously dispose the Pharisaic sect to a coalition with Christ on the ground of their common national and theocratic feeling; he might become a useful friend in the metropolis, and might fight against the prejudice which a provincial and Galilaean party could not but excite. These advantages Christ would secure by allowing Nicodemus to become a secret member of his theocracy, and by excusing him, until a better opportunity should present itself, from publicly undergoing the rite of baptism. On the other hand, by insisting upon this he would at once destroy all the influence of Nicodemus with the authorities of Jerusalem, and with it all his power of becoming a nursing-father to the infant church.

When we consider the great contempt which Christ constantly expressed for forms and ceremonies, and in particular for those "washings" which were usual among the Pharisees, we are prepared to find him readily acceding to the request of Nicodemus. Instead, he shut the petitioner's mouth by an abrupt declaration that there was no way into the kingdom but through baptism. The kingdom of God, he insisted, though it had no locality and no separation from the secular states of mankind, though it had no law courts, no lictors and no fasces, was yet a true state. Men were not to make a light thing of entering it, to give their names to the Founder at a secret interview and immediately return to their accustomed places of resort to take up the routine of secular life where it had been left. Those who would enroll themselves among its citizens were to understand that they began their life anew, as truly as if they had been born again. And lest the Divine Society, in its contempt for material boundaries and for the distinctiveness which is given by unity of place, should lose its distinctiveness altogether and degenerate into a theory or a sentiment or a devout imagination, the initiatory rite of baptism, with its publicity and formality, was pronounced as indispensable to membership as that spiritual inspiration which is membership itself.

Baptism being thus indispensable, we may be surprised to find it so seldom mentioned in the accounts of Christ's life. We do not read, for example, of the baptism of his principal disciples. But it is to be remembered that the rite of baptism, though used by Christ, was not introduced by him, and that he recognized the theocracy as having begun to exist in a rudimentary form before his own public appearance. The work of John was merged in that of Christ as a river in the sea, but Christ regards those who had received John's baptism as being already members of the kingdom. Since the time of John, he says, the kingdom of heaven suffereth violence, and the violent take it by force. Now Christ's first followers were likely to be drawn from John's circle—partly because John himself directed his followers to Christ, partly because those who were affected by the eloquency of the one prophet were naturally formed to fall under the influence of the other. That the fact actually was so is attested by our biographies, which distinctly speak of Christ as finding his earliest disciples in the neighborhood and among the followers of the Baptist. This being the case, we may presume that the bulk of the first Christians received baptism from John and found themselves already enrolled in a society, the objects of which neither they nor perhaps the Baptist himself clearly understood, before they had ever seen the fact of Christ.

The Acts of the Apostles afford many proofs that the first Christians regarded John's disciples as members of the church, but imperfectly instructed.

• • •

John had described Jesus as the "Lamb of God, which taketh away the sin of the world." Jesus was blessed by an unrivaled simplicity of devout confidence in God. After the incidents surrounding his baptism, with possibly considerable agitation of mind, he is led by the Spirit into the wilderness to be with his Father. The consciousness that now he was fully commissioned to begin his public ministry and the fact that he was conscious of miraculous power combined to make it necessary for him to undergo the fasting discipline in the lonely places. While none of the Gospels point this out specifically, the use of his powers over nature is visibly the key to the whole episode. What is called Christ's temptation is evidently the excitement of mind caused by his consciousness of possession of supernatural power. How shall it be used? Upon what principles is it to be handled, and upon what occasions is it to be displayed?

After his communion with God, Jesus finds himself in a barren waste without food. His prolonged fast had taken its toll. He was hungry. With the hunger comes the temptation: "If thou be the Son of God, command these stones to be made bread!" Simply the power to do this constituted this temptation. The possession of special power always constitutes the greatest temptation with which a virtuous man may be asssailed. In difficult circumstances few men can wield extraordinary power without becoming corrupt. But Jesus here, alone, gifted with supernatural power, was thrown completely upon the instinct of virtue within him.

His response to the voice of the tempter is most extraordinary. He is not elated by the knowledge of his supernatural gifts; he is, rather, awe-stricken. He refuses to use for himself that which he regards as a sacred trust committed to him for the good of others. In his own extreme need he suffers rather than help himself from resources placed in his hands to further the kingdom of God. Was ever such self-denial as this? In his triumphant victory he showed himself Lord of the flesh.

There is a further aspect to this. His countrymen were looking for a time of plenty—a feast of fat things. Christ knew that men would follow one who gave them bread. But he knew, too, that the kingdom could not rest on such a shallow foundation. Men must be won by love and gratitude or their service would prove ultimately worthless. And how penetrating his answer: "Man shall not live by bread alone, but by every word that proceedeth out of the mouth of God."

Jesus was now taken by the Spirit to the pinnacle of the Temple. In the exhilaration which was his as he overcame the first temptation he now found himself tempted to show wonder to the multitude. Men will follow mystery, and the naked display of power always fascinates them. Should he use his power in this way to recruit disciples to his cause? Christ knew that to doubt his Father's protective providence was treason and there was no need to put it to a test. "Throw thyself down," said the tempter. "For it is written, He shall give his angels charge over thee, and in their hands they shall bear thee up." To no other person perhaps could this temptation have occurred.

The third temptation may not be easy to understand. A vision of universal monarchy rose before him. What suggested such things to the son of the carpenter? Only the sense of supernatural power which had tempted him to turn the stone into bread, and after that to throw himself from the Temple.

The consciousness of this power coupled with the Baptist's predictions, and the Messianic prophecies of past times on which Jesus had thought much, combined to suggest this possibility of universal monarchy. He pictured himself enthroned in Jerusalem with Rome paying tribute to him. There was one condition, however. "All these will I give thee," said the tempter, "if thou wilt fall down and worship me."

The Zealots were waiting for the Messiah. They would gladly lay down their lives in mortal combat if only the kingdom thereby might come. All Christ had to do was use on their behalf this strange supernatural power, and victory over Rome—indeed the independence of the whole Jewish nation from every creature beneath the celestial world—would be abundantly assured. Jesus was tempted to employ force in the establishment of his kingdom. He must have heard from those who taught him earlier in life that the Messiah was to put all enemies under his feet and to crush all opposition by God-given might.

This was the general expectation among the people. And it was precisely because he steadily refused to do this that his countrymen finally rejected him. "It was not only," says Sir J. Seeley, "that they expected a king and he appeared only as a teacher; he systematically described himself as a king. To them the stumbling block was this, that, professing to be a king, he declined to use the weapons of force and compulsion that belong to kings." It is quite to be accepted that Jesus would have had a struggle within himself, knowing that he would have to run counter to the hopes and expectations of his contemporaries.

There is no doubt that it would have been possible for Jesus thus to have established himself in the regalia of earthly kings. All men would have been subject to him. Fear of consequences of disloyalty would have kept them falsely true. But such a course would have produced only another kingdom of this world. It would have been powerless to change the hearts and dispositions of men. Jesus deliberately chose another and an infinitely more difficult course. He would win the consent of men and build his kingdom on that. He knew such consent would have to be won through a display of his mighty love and terrible purity. He resolved that no matter how bitterly they might persecute him he would use his supernatural power only in blessing them and doing good.

He persevered in this course even though it was politically disastrous, and baffled his closest followers. By doing so he raised himself to a throne in men's hearts where he has been seated for almost two thousand years and gained ascendency and authority over men greater than they have allowed anyone else—greater even than prophecy itself ever attributed to the Messiah.

Christ would still win us by his love and sacrifice. He would have us serve him out of love and gratitude. Indeed there is no other acceptable way of Christian service. It is the combination of greatness and self-sacrifice which wins our hearts, the mighty powers held under restraint, the unspeakable condescension— which issued in the Cross of Christ. The Cross was the fruit of Christ's victory in those hours of temptation in the wilderness.

• • •

To what extent John and Jesus were identified in the latter's early ministry it is difficult to say. The two movements were really one, and the river of John's work flowed naturally into the ocean of the proclamation of the Christ. It must have been with deep and profound regret that Jesus learned of the death of the Baptist.

It would be hard to exaggerate the influence of John on the life of the Master. John's preaching had initiated the sense of divine calling, and his imprisonment was the event which sent Jesus out on his public ministry with passionate purpose. Henceforth Jesus must work alone. He must forego the association of his cousin.

Jesus apparently did not begin to preach immediately following the wilderness temptation, nor did he return at once to Galilee. The arrest of John made it necessary for him to begin his own public ministry. As he came into Galilee, he proclaimed his message which was basically threefold in character. First he proclaimed that "the time is at hand." He did not seem to dwell on the glorious deeds of the heroes of the past; he did not delve into the future even as much as John seemed to do. Instead he spoke of the present. "The time," he said, "is fulfilled." He preached that the kingdom of heaven was "at hand," and said, "Repent ye and believe the gospel." The past is gone—irretrievably gone. The future is tenuous. Only the living, vital present is relevant.

This is always true. The good news of the Gospel always begins with the movement of God in the present time.

The second aspect of his ministry which appeared at the beginning was his deliberate seeking and calling of individual men. There is no reason to suppose that when Jesus called Simon, Andrew, James, and John they were seeing him for the first time. But the wonder and amazement is that when he called, they answered affirmatively. The call was uttered in complete confidence. "Come," he said, "and I will make you fishers of men." It was answered without hesitation; "And they left their nets and followed him."

The choice of disciples was not a passing incident. They were chosen to be the instruments through whom the divine kingdom was to be established. Jesus wrote no books but he did write himself into the lives of the disciples, and these were his interpreters. His life was their light and he dedicated himself to the emergence and growth of his own image in them. Perhaps this is the greatest evidence of his courage, that he selected these men to share his life and ministry and, finally, his death.

Jesus needed these disciples for purposes other than the perpetuation of his ministry. He chose them "that they might be with him." Can we not see that he chose them for himself? And that he needed them so they could give that sympathetic companionship and quiet understanding upon which, in times of discouragement, he might fall back and find some measure of renewal. Can we not see that he needs us too?

The third aspect of Christ's early ministry, which remained constant throughout his whole endeavor, was the art of healing. It is not according to the record to stress the teaching of Jesus and not place equal stress upon his gift of healing. He released men and women from suffering. He was not merely a teacher, or a leader, or a healer; he was all three—all the time. The Gospels record, time and time again, how Jesus healed bodily affliction simply out of his compassion for people.

Occasionally we seem to note the limitation on the power of Jesus to heal where faith was lacking in those around him: "He could do no mighty works, because of their unbelief." Again, in one passage of Matthew, Jesus is represented, as in the other Synoptists, as transmitting to his disciples the power to work miracles of healing, as notice a heightening of the picture: "Heal the sick, raise the dead, cleanse the leper, cast out devils. Freely ye have received, freely give," where Mark refers only to healing generally and mentions particularly the method of anointing. But this heightening of the miraculous coloring is not discoverable generally or to any considerable extent. The picture is substantially identical in all the Synoptic Gospels. Owing indeed to the fewness of the discourses of Jesus recorded by Mark, the picture of the miraculous worker is in higher relief in his narrative than in any of the other Gospels. But in all of them the authority to work miracles and the spiritual

112

authority to teach and to forgive are represented as inseparable the one from the other. Here is a real man, but a real man endowed with the authority of God, morally and physically. This is the irresistible impression.

In all the Gospels we note the relatively subordinate evidential position assigned to the wonderful works of Jesus. He was no mere wonder-worker, though he worked wonders. This is made evident in the account of his temptation. He would not obtain belief by dazzling men. Jesus knew the worthlessness of such belief. "If they hear not Moses and the prophets, neither will they be persuaded," in any real spiritual sense, by a supernatural occurrence. This appears to be the interpretation of our Lord's stern refusal to meet the demand of the scribes and Pharisees for a "sign" or a "sign from heaven"—some public demonstration of miraculous power on a great scale wrought to prove demonstratively his divine authority. This he would not give.

His miracles were incidental. They issued from a pity which knew that it had power to heal men's sicknesses and supply their physical needs, and could not refrain from using it; but they were rather concealed than advertised; or they were elements in the training of the disciples to trust him utterly; or if occasionally they were intended to serve, like the healing of the paralytic man, as proofs to the eye of the spiritual authority which he claimed, they were still incidental or unpremeditated, and in the presence of a relatively small company.

We would see Jesus, with the eye of faith,

in his work of healing, in his matchless leadership of men, and on the mountain teaching. Still, as of old, he calls, "Follow me."

• • •

And immediately he left the synagogue, and entered the house of Simon and Andrew, with James and John. Now Simon's mother-in-law lay sick with a fever, and immediately they told him of her. And he came and took her by the hand and lifted her up, and the fever left her; and she served them.

That evening at sundown, they brought to him all who were sick or possessed with demons. And the whole city was gathered together about the door. And he healed many who were sick with various diseases, and cast out many demons; and he would not permit the demons to speak, because they knew him.

And in the morning, a great while before day, he rose and went out to a lonely place, and there he prayed. And Simon and those who were with him followed him, and they found him and said unto him, "Everyone is searching for you." And he said to them, "Let us go on to the next towns, that I may preach there also; for that is why I came out." And he went throughout all Galilee, preaching in their synagogues and casting out demons.—Mark 1:29 ff.

Jesus was a man of prayer. The habit must have been formed at his mother's knee and continued with him until he uttered the sigh of peace, "Father, into thy hands I commend my spirit." The unique communion of Jesus with his Father seems to have been instinctive. Jesus grew to maturity in the consciousness of the Divine Presence. His countrymen believed in prayer, he discovered, but they had very little actual communion with God. Their lives were off-center; God had second or

114

third place in their lives. So there were many sick among them.

It is difficult to assess what the phrase "possessed of demons" actually means. Many people in our own day seem to be driven by forces which they neither understand nor control. Whatever terminology we use is not so important as the fact that in his infinite concern Christ healed all manner of diseases. How this occurred we can only conjecture. Jesus did change the lives of many people who had warped and twisted personalities, and by the contagion of his own person gave them the assurance of divine care and protection. Christ's concern was not only for the nation in general but for the needs of individuals as well. Christ's earliest followers came from common homes and in these common homes common illness frequently occurred. So, then, after the service at the Synagogue, Jesus went to the home of Simon and healed his wife's mother. Knowledge of this miracle naturally spread, and others came until the "whole city was gathered at the door."

So much had he given of himself that he felt keenly the need of being alone in prayer. He forsook the needy people temporarily, not because he did not care for them but because even in his life the inner springs needed to be renewed.

The background of the life of the Master was one of prayer. Long before the opening of his public ministry, Jesus had formed the habit of sharing intimacies with his Father and of working out his growing problems in the constant light of his Father's presence. Prayer, therefore, naturally entered into the outstanding events of his later life.

At his baptism, the prayer of Jesus was followed by an immediate endowment (Luke 3:21, 22). On another occasion shortly afterward, although he had been busy until late at night with the ministry of healing, he rose before day and went to a solitary place that he might find refreshment in prayer, and as a result he returned with renewed urgency to the preaching of the word (Luke 1:33). Later still, when the growing opposition of the priests and the unwieldy spiritual inertia of the mass of the people forced him to select a more intimate circle of disciples, "that they might be with him," he spent the night in prayer before choosing the twelve (Luke 6:12).

On that supremely significant day when he tested the growing understanding of his disciples by asking them what men said about him, and in reply received from Peter the assurance of the confirmation of God as to his divinity, he had come to them from a night of prayer (Luke 9:18). At still another time, when he sought the fellowship of his friends in that communion which had proved so fruitful in his own life and retired to the mountain with Peter, James, and John, his prayer life led to his transfiguration.

The greater his need and the more insistent the demands upon him, the more apparent is his utter reliance upon his Father and his eagerness to do his Father's work. No incident in the whole of his ministry is more revealing than his prayer before Gethsemane (John 17) or the later communion with his Father whenever his disciples had failed him (Luke 22:40, 41).

In the life of Jesus, prayer was thinking things through with God, and into this thinking came a sense of adoration and dependence. As he trained the disciples, Jesus sought to inspire in them a similar desire and ability to think things through from the divine point of view. Put into modern English, one of his complaints to Peter was, "You think like a man when you ought to think like God" (Luke 8:3). When talking with the Pharisees, he said (in modern terms), "You do not think in God's way; therefore your lives are out of focus" (Luke 16:15).

On his first missionary trip through Galilee Jesus preached the gospel of repentance, which had been the theme of his predecessor, John the Baptist. But the richer and deeper spiritual experience of the Master revealed itself in the larger meaning he gave to repentance. To him it was not merely a negative philosophy, but was wholly constructive. It meant rethinking from the changed vantage point of the man who gives God his place at the heart of affairs. To Jesus, the kingdoms of the world were of small importance compared with the kingdom of God, and learning to think God's way was the foundation of his kingdom.

With Jesus, this practice of thinking things through with God was not solely an intellectual process. To him, the very heart of such evaluation was recognition of the Divine Nature—the knowledge that God is love. All Jesus' thought and prayer placed this outstanding fact of love first. He did not need to approach each problem with the question in his mind, "How would my Father solve this?" He did not have to remind himself continually in solving this problem or that, "I must remember that God is love." The habit of taking God into his counsel and of recognizing the divine love was part of his whole life. It had become habitual.

God is interested in men. He so loved the world that he "gave his only begotten Son" (John 3:16) that they might achieve abundant and eternal life. God loves the sparrows (Matthew 6:20), and the grass growing in wondrous beauty on the hillsides but tomorrow burned as stubble in the ovens. How much more does God love men and women! If we ask him, would he not give us the bread of life? (Matthew 6:28-30).

The fact that Jesus prayed so often is of tremendous significance to us. He had a sense of need. He was humble. He actually revealed God, the Father, to us, but the fact that he prayed indicates he was not God the Father. He was never self-sufficient and that fact makes us sure of his divine vocation. Is it not significant to us that he felt the need of prayer? How can we ever hope to overcome ourselves in our own strength if the great overcomer of all relied solely on his Father? The fact that Christ prayed makes his life more relevant to ours, because prayer is something that he and we have in common.

● ● ●

As Jesus began to extend his ministry two things became apparent. First, he found that the masses were unable to appreciate his teachings. The people were shortsighted and fickle, following after the loaves and fishes, and bringing their sick for healing but utterly unable or unwilling to understand the beauty and power of his teaching. Second, he met with increasing hostility from the religious leaders. His only recourse, therefore, was to choose a small band of followers who, by more intimate contact with him, could be trained to carry on his mission.

Jesus chose the Twelve and they came with full purpose of heart to take his name upon them. They did not choose him; he chose them. He trained them and in fellowship finally bestowed the secret of the great mystery upon them. "Whom do *men* say that I am?" was only leading up to "Whom say *ye* that I am?" So God addresses each one sooner or later. That question must be answered in every life. The fate of the individual and the fate of nations depend on the answer they give. Eventually God confronts all men in Jesus.

The apostolic answer is given by Peter and it is a gift of the Spirit: "Thou art the Christ, the Son of the living God." "No man calleth Jesus Lord but by the Holy Ghost." "To some it is given by the Holy Ghost to *know* that Jesus is the Son of God, and that he was crucified for the sins of the world." This knowledge comes only to those who desire to take upon them the name of the Christ "with full purpose of heart," for this desire is part of the gift—"He gave some apostles."

God set in the church "first, apostles." Apostleship

is a gift—the basic gift, a gift of the Spirit—and upon it the church is built. Anyone who has this knowledge is in that sense an apostle. This knowledge requires of those who possess it that they *bear witness*. With the gift comes the longing to testify—based on the love of Jesus Christ. To know him is to know oneself and all men truly. This revelation of the Spirit unlocks the mystery of man's nature.

Today we are beset by many theories of the nature of man and the reasons for his behavior. Freud challenges us with his concept of repression and his theories of human nature based upon psychoanalysis. Jung has delved into the collective unconscious and regaled us with his doctrine of archetypes. Rank asserts that all history is intelligible as man's protest against death—as his striving for immortality. Theories of education, based on doctrines of man's nature, have gone through their gyrations. We shall ceaselessly search for the true meaning of human nature until Jesus reveals himself to us and then will our search be ended.

Man, left to himself and to nature, cannot know God truly. Left to himself, man does not know himself either, for only in the knowledge of God does man know himself. For, "He knoweth our frame; he remembereth that we are dust." This knowledge of God and man is the revelation of Christ as the Son of God, crucified for the sins of the world; a gift, the first gift of the Spirit. How wise was the apostle who wrote: "I determined not to know anything among you, save Jesus Christ, and him crucified."

A significant prophetic insight was expressed by

Jesus who, when beholding Peter for the first time, said to him: "Thou art Simon the son of Jona: thou shalt be called Cephas, which is by interpretation, a seer, or a stone." Our Lord was looking toward the great Confession at Caesarea Philippi and beyond, when Peter would be given the apostolic gift and sent out to testify. Thus Peter by this gift was to be likened to the Urim and Thummim, the stone set in Israel through which was revealed the will of God. It was upon this rock, the rock of the revelation of God in Christ, that the church was to be built. Peter evidently never forgot this reference made by Jesus to himself. Years later he wrote to the church: "Ye also, as lively stones [as stones alive with the will of God], are built up a spiritual house, an holy priesthood."

Some of the pen portraits consist of just a few lines but how revealing they are! Philip, for instance, was so unimpressive personally that he is introduced to us merely as a native of the same town as Andrew and Peter. Yet it was he who found Nathaniel, and the simple words, "Come and see," show how powerful is the word of testimony even from unobtrusive lives. Then there were the two Jameses. One of them was called "James the less"—not a very distinguished appellation. In the Greek it is rendered "the tiny one." Yet he found place in the Twelve alongside the others. James and John, the sons of "thunder," were there too, with Simon the Zealot who hated the Romans, and Matthew, a Roman tax-gatherer. Judas Iscariot bore the proud name of the greatest of the Maccabbeans, which later he disgraced. Then there was

Thomas, the doubter, who had to be shown. These and others were the good men whose various personalities Jesus molded as the means of sending the Good News into all the world.

The apostles frequently misunderstood their Master's world-shaking message, but they paid a price to become his disciples. Peter told him once, "Lo, we have left all to follow thee."

"Earth has its price," says Sir Launfal, "for what earth gives." So does the kingdom. Discipleship is not easy, but it is glorious.

● ● ●

It seems that the first public appearance of Jesus was in his hometown of Nazareth. He appeared "as his custom was," says Luke, in the synagogue. The synagogue had no regular minister, but in the seats on the platform sat the chief and a number of the leading elders. The person in charge might call on anyone of suitable age and reliable character to read out of the Law and the Prophets and comment as he might choose. News of the miracles of Jesus at nearby Cana had preceded him; this probably explains why he was chosen for reading and comments. He stood and read from Isaiah; the reading finished, he sat down to teach and the congregation stood to receive instruction.

His comments had to do with the coming Messiah and were essentially a declaration of his own purpose and program. At first, "all bore him witness and wondered at the gracious words which proceeded

122

out of his mouth." Then as the Master continued he quoted:

> He hath anointed me to preach the
>   gospel to the poor.
> He hath sent me to heal the brokenhearted,
> To preach deliverance to the captives,
> And recovering of sight to the blind,
> To set at liberty them that are bruised.
> To preach the acceptable year of the
>   Lord.

As Jesus watched he saw resentment gradually appear upon the faces of his audience. Evidently, to them, he meant that the blessings of God were to be bestowed on Jew and Gentile alike. The implication of this struck straight across the lives of their narrow nationalism. "What right has Joseph's son to talk this way?" they asked. Jesus did not recede from his position, but went on further to quote from the Scriptures some of the incidents where the goodness of God was freely given to those not of Israel. Then frowns increased and their resentful mutterings mounted to a roar of disapproval. Some would have flung him down from the hilltop and stoned him. But Jesus passed through their midst and went to Capernaum where the following Sabbath found him in the synagogue preaching the same doctrine.

As long as Jesus was content to be one of the common people he was widely and popularly known. His fellow townsmen even rejoiced in his apparent success at Jerusalem and in Samaria and at Cana. But when the very qualities which first commended Jesus to the approval of the Nazarenes led him beyond the limitations of their understanding and their vision, they had to recognize his greatness or find shelter behind indignant denunciation of his presumption. With a humanness which we can readily understand, they chose the latter. To accept Jesus involved renunciations they were entirely unwilling to make. Loving their own sense of special privilege more than they loved truth and righteousness, they cast the Master out from their midst.

Capernaum was quite a cosmopolitan city, and the people were free from many of the narrow prejudices which blinded the Nazarenes. It was also a major political and commercial center, and for these and other reasons Jesus henceforth made it the hub of his work in Galilee.

In Capernaum and the region round about, those who saw and heard Jesus were amazed at his quiet but clear authority: "They were astonished at his doctrine: for he taught them as one that had authority, and not as the scribes." He greatly preferred to state the facts about God and about the kingdom and the conditions of citizenship in the kingdom rather than to enter into theological disputations. Nor did he depend on the writings of the spiritual leaders of the past to reinforce his authority as the scribes and Pharisees did. He never subordinated his authority to any of those who had gone before. On his lips old phrases, therefore, came to have new meaning; ancient truth was made to glow with living power; and the message of the prophets was sent forth once again with new wisdom and new light.

With Capernaum as his base of operations, Jesus extended his ministry throughout the neighboring countryside, preaching and healing. On these trips into the country, and also during the intervals in Capernaum, the Master steadily enriched the lives of his disciples. Many of these, like Andrew, Peter, James, and John, had been disciples of John the Baptist before they followed the Master. Others, like Matthew, may first have heard the good news of the kingdom from the lips of Jesus himself. This period was therefore important for its influence both in the community and in the personal and social lives of those who were nearest to Jesus.

At the beginning of his ministry the scribes and Pharisees regarded Jesus with the superciliousness which they tended to manifest toward those not of their particular circle. Then, as Jesus emerged as a person of much greater consequence than they had first realized, the hostility of these leaders crystallized and became more and more apparent.

The heart of the difficulty lay in the determination of the leaders of Judaism to perpetuate Hebrew institutions rather than to achieve a better way of life. They were the conservers of the status quo. They were not all necessarily selfish nor ambitious for power, although some of their number certainly had both of these limitations, but they conceived religion as something static and, by restricting themselves to observance of the "law of carnal commandments," failed to rise to the spiritual heights. So sure were they of the essential rightness of their procedure that they regarded anyone who differed from them as a menace to their temporal and eternal well-being, and they actually used their concern for spiritual things as an argument to justify the cruelty they used to suppress freedom of thought and action.

The wide cleavage between Jesus and the scribes and Pharisees is illustrated by the objections raised by the latter when Jesus ate with "publicans and sinners." The rulers simply could not understand this. They felt that it indicated a loose indulgence toward sin, and if it was encouraged, such indiscriminate friendliness would break down the moral fiber of the nation. Jesus told them, "They that are whole have no need of the physician, but they that are sick: I came not to call the righteous, but sinners to repentance." But the scribes and Pharisees continued in their blind prejudice. They made obedience to the law and tradition ends in themselves, while Jesus insisted that these must minister to an inner, spiritual growth.

When Jesus set himself against entrenched interests no compromise was possible. From that time forward, Jesus was doomed. Early in his ministry the lines of conflict were drawn. Although they killed Jesus, they made alive thereby the gospel they hated.

● ● ●

The idea of the kingdom did not begin with the earthly ministry of Jesus. Long before his day the prophets had foretold the time when "the mountain of the Lord's house" should be established "in the tops of the mountains" and all nations should flow into it. All classes of Hebrew people were eagerly awaiting a new day when Jesus appeared on the scene.

126

Joseph of Arimathea was "looking for the kingdom of God." Simeon hoped for the "consolation of Israel," and Anna is described as one who was looking for the "redemption of Jerusalem." The eyes of most other nations looked backward. The Jews looked forward, taught to do so by the prophets. But none of the common people were very clear about the "kingdom of heaven" or the "consolation of Israel." They knew, somehow, that these terms stood for a new social order based on response to the divine rule.

The Zealots, for instance, looked for an earthly kingdom to be founded, if necessary, by force. The Pharisees, for the largest group, knew there was little hope of a military victory against the might of Rome. They looked for a miraculous demonstration of divine power by which their enemies would be overthrown. Such miraculous outpouring they felt would come in response to punctilious observance of the legal code. Still another group believed that by gradual moral perfection of the lives of the Hebrews they would be so elevated above the people of their times as to enable them to dominate the earth.

So when Jesus began preaching he did so to people who had differing conceptions of the kingdom. The phrase meant one thing to him and another to them. They placed their emphasis on "the kingdom" while he placed his on "of God." They longed only for their emancipation from Rome and to be first among the nations. His idea was to make God's will more fully revealed among the people and done on earth as it is in heaven.

His vision of the kingdom demanded the emergence of a Messiah who would fit the description of "the Lamb of God." Their understanding led them to expect a very different type of deliverer.

Jesus was tied irrevocably to the past.

His mind is saturated with the ideas of the Old Testament; his language is learned from its phraseology; the figures of the Patriarchs and the pious kings occupy his imagination; and he knows himself to be the successor and heir of the prophets. If the Kingdom of God was the underlying idea of the whole Old Testament history, this was the best reason for its being the prominent watchword of his preaching.—Stalker, *The Ethics of Jesus*, p. 47.

To Jesus, the term kingdom of God expressed the essential relation between himself and his followers. John had been the herald of the kingdom. Jesus was the King. All the rights of the people are conserved and guaranteed in the kingdom of God, but it is not a democracy. It is the realm in which the will of God is supreme. Jesus made his major appeal to the Jews. He preached in the synagogues in Galilee and then when he went to Jerusalem he went to the temple and dealt with the heads of the Jewish community. If the Jews rejected him, that meant he had not been received by "his own."

The apostles too, when they were sent out to preach, were commanded to address their ministry to the "lost sheep of the house of Israel." They knew they were part of a struggle between a people who were unwilling to live up to the high standards of their calling and the One who had called them. The struggle came to a climax when Pilate asked of them, "Shall I crucify your king?" and the chief priests truly answered, "We have no king but Caesar."

Jesus never defined the kingdom. Formal definitions have a way of becoming the occasion of formal hair-splitting, and had he given such definition men would have been arguing about it from that day to this. Instead he set before men pathways to discovery. If men would express eagerness to know about the kingdom let them adventure along these pathways. He told them rather what the kingdom was like: leaven hidden in a measure of meal, hidden treasure, a merchant seeking a goodly pearl, like growing seed or like the ten virgins five of whom were wise and the other five foolish. It is difficult to find any aspect of nature which did not testify to the Master and minister to his growing assurance of the kingdom of his Father.

Had we learned to discern this testimony in the ordinary things of life, as he did, our lives today would have been immeasurably enriched.

Jesus was definite about one thing. The kingdom was primarily God's gift to men. It can be built only as men seek to cooperate with him.

"No one can assist in this work, except he be humble and full of love." The key word here is *assist*. Jesus put his finger on this most primary of all phases of the kingdom in his pattern-prayer. *Thine* is the kingdom and the power and the glory for *ever and ever*. It belongs to him in a way it can never belong to us.

The keynote of the kingdom proclaimed by Christ is loyalty to the God of righteousness and service to all mankind. It still is. Whenever the kingdom is built it will be by him and with the cooperation of those who love and serve him without qualification or regret. Without him, we cannot build it. Without us he will not.

● ● ●

Just prior to Gethsemane and Calvary there came to pass in the life of Jesus a series of incidents which reflect what he expects of his followers. They emphasize and reemphasize the social aspects of his message. He knew he was nearing the end of his earthly work, when he would leave his disciples and return to his Father. He had, in his life and word, displayed the glory of his Father's kingdom and yet they, in their own humor and blindness, did not understand.

The first day of the feast of unleavened bread found the disciples and their Master just outside Jerusalem. The feast was closely connected in time and in importance to the great feast of the Passover, and Jesus was reminded of the necessary preparations for the event. Not only this but he had great desire to eat this Passover with them—the last before he had to suffer.

This "desire" was stimulated by a number of things, among them his past associations with his beloved, his knowledge through his prescience that this would be his last Passover, and also the knowledge that before him was the task of giving to his disciples and all the Christian world the sublimation of the Passover and the lessons which were crowded into the time of the Passover Supper and the initiation of the Lord's Supper.

At this point we will let Dr. Frederick M. Smith take up the chronicle of events.

He sent two of his most trusted disciples to prepare the room, the feast, and for their reception when they should come later. But they failed him to a degree, and in that failure they gave Jesus opportunity for an important lesson. They found the room, prepared it, killed the lamb, and spread the feast. But for the reception of their Master and their brethren there was not adequate preparation made.

The reason of their failure lies at the bottom of a trait often displayed by man. It is said in the Scriptures that there had been strife among the disciples, even those closest to Jesus. They could not agree which of them should be accounted the greatest. With the bitterness that always is a concomitant of such strife, one of the social amenities was omitted from the reception of Jesus and the brethren at the room of the feast.

In those times and in that country, the common footgear, where footgear was worn at all, was the sandal. The soil being sandy and rocky, a great discomfort to the traveler was the accumulation of sand and pebbles between the sandal and foot; and between the toes. So one of the first acts of hospitality extended to an incoming guest by a host was for a basin of water and towel to be brought, and the feet laved, so the foot-weariness and irritation by sand and pebble could be relieved and the guest enter in comfort. This act of courtesy was usually done by a servant, of course at the command or by instruction of the host, or as a result of his previous training. It was a custom well established.

But the disciples, already quarreling as to which of them was the greatest, were unwilling to assume the role of a servant and refresh the incoming guest by an act of hospitality so much needed. Apparently, on coming to the room Jesus took little or no notice of this error on the part of those he had sent to make preparations, but after they had eaten, and probably after he had listened to the rumblings of the strife as to the greatest, and mayhap even about the question of washing of feet, he arose, girded himself with a towel (a sign or symbol of a servant), took a basin of water, and he himself washed the feet of his disciples. Then he at once impressed a beautiful lesson of service and administered a stern rebuke to his disciples for their discourtesy.

When he had finished and had taken his garments and sat down, he asked them if they knew what he had done to them. He said: "Ye call me Master, and Lord; and ye say well; for so I am. If I then, your Lord and Master, have washed your feet; ye also ought to wash one another's feet. For I have *given you an example*, that ye should do as I have done to you. Verily, verily, I say unto you, the servant is not greater than his lord; neither he that is sent greater than he that sent him."

No finer demonstration of the principle of real service could be given than this incident. No question arose in the mind of the Master as to class or station of those needing service. His only question was, "Is service needed?" And his answer to that has given the Christian world a fine example. An *example* it was, not a *pattern*. Here, as in many other cases of events related in the Bible, certain things have been taken out of their proper setting, and made to do service where not intended. Jesus, in order to impress the lesson of service to those in need, and to attend to what should have been done when the guests arrived at the room of the feast, himself washed the feet of the disciples, as an *example*, and did not intend it as the pattern of a ceremony to be perpetuated, as some have tried to do. What he meant, as I believe, when he said, "an example, that ye should do as I have done to you," was when there is service to do, acts of kindness to render, courtesies to extend, the question of rank, caste, or class should not be raised, but ministry rendered without question; and that in such ministry, the master, the great, would in no way suffer degradation, but would be honored for his spirit of kindness and helpfulness.

There is no need today, when man's feet are more protectingly shod, for the courtesy of foot-washing at the door; but there is always need for distress to be relieved, kindness to be extended, and graciousness to be manifested.

How is it with you? Do you withhold your ministry of goodness at times because in your opinion persons are below you in rank? Who draws the lines of rank, anyhow? And who will draw them at the great and final bar of judgment?

Thus the great Master of men administered a rebuke to his disciples and demonstrated his own humility. When one reflects upon the gods of the philosophers he does not find among them such self-effacing humility. Our heavenly Father was among us once in Jesus Christ, and was among us as "One who served." We are made that eventually we may become like he is. Our opportunity to do so lies in our service to those in need.

• • •

In the upper chamber where Jesus and his disciples assembled to eat the Passover, there occurred two dramas which have tremendous significance for all Christians. One was the betrayal of Jesus by Judas Iscariot and the other consisted in the giving by Jesus to his disciples the new commandment. The Passover was one of the greatest of the feasts of the Jews and so remains among all who observe it and the Hebraic laws. Jesus well knew its significance historically and its social value as well as he did its religious import. In that room was to be instituted a ceremony which would supplant the Passover for his followers—and afterwards was to be enacted the sacrifice which would forever sublimate the Passover. The Lord's Supper became a preparation for Gethsemane and Calvary which followed.

We have noted his lesson of service, exemplified by washing the feet of his apostles. After they had eaten the Passover, he blessed bread and gave it to them to eat as emblematic of his body broken for them, and wine as emblematic of his shed blood. This was the first Lord's Supper, superseding among all Christians the feast of the Passover. And the Lord's Supper continues to be celebrated as one of the sacraments. Among us of the Reorganized Church of Jesus Christ of Latter Day Saints, it constitutes each time, if properly partaken of, a renewal of the covenant made in the waters of baptism, a promise to obey the Christian mandates.

Who of us can sense the deep grief of Jesus when Judas Iscariot left the upper chamber on his trip of betrayal? The record of the happenings in the room makes no mention of his sorrow, except perhaps a faint indication of it; but as Jesus knew beforehand who would betray him, and the time, he probably had suffered in *anticipation* and had conquered the outward manifestations of his keen grief. But who can doubt that this was one of the factors which later impelled him to seek Gethsemane and plead for the passing of the cruel cup.

The betrayal by Judas of his Master is a grim commentary on the fact that agency is ultimate. It cannot be doubted that Jesus knew who was to betray him, and he appears to have made one last desperate appeal to Judas when he selected the bread and dipped it into the wine and gave it to him. The Scriptures record that immediately after the sop, "Satan entered into him." Jesus, however, who knew what was to take place not only kept silence but protected Judas with the words, "That thou doest, do quickly." We do not know whether Peter had his sword with him in the chamber, but he certainly had it with him in the Garden of Gethsemane. What might have happened had Peter known the intention of Judas to betray the Master? So Judas passed out into the night with the protection of the Master.

We are not here watching the dealings of one man with another. We are looking at the way in which God deals with men. If a man will betray the Son of God, then the heavenly mandate is, "So be it." God is made to serve with their sins, according to the tremendous words of Isaiah. But even more than this, this is the way the kingdom of God meets the sin of the world. God takes the worst that wicked men and nations can do, suffers their violence, and yet, in the end, turns their tragic sins to a revelation of his own glory, such as was manifest upon the cross.

There has been almost endless debate upon the fate or the ultimate condition of the soul of Judas. We do know that he was overcome with remorse. The motives of Judas and the possible reason for his conduct are beyond the scope of this talk. But the tremendous and all encompassing truth is that agency, or the power of choice, is a gift of God, vouchsafed in our creation, and God himself is subject to it. He dare not violate the law of man's own being. He is limited in his capacity to bless and redeem us by the fact that we have agency, and that this gift of

God to us has imposed limitations on him, which he himself has ordained.

There is no doubt that Christ could have restrained Judas. The fact that he did not speaks volumes about God and man and their relation, the one to the other. Love may make its appeal to us. It does so in a myriad number of ways, most of all in the vision of that august and awe-inspiring symbol of the divine supremacy, the dreadful yet beauteous solitude of the Master upon the cross. And yet we may, and often do, refuse love's appeal. Love and its attendant sacrifice is the only known relationship or procedure in the universe that will change a man's will and yet conserve his freedom. For it is in acts of sacrifice in which what we want is renounced for the sake of someone loved that we are most conscious of being supremely free.

After Judas had in anger left the room there occurred one of the important events which transpired in that room, now matchless in its historic importance. Turning to his disciples Christ addressed them as "little children," saying he would be with them yet a little while, that he would go where they could not come. He addressed them as children, for even after their years of experience with him, sitting under his instruction, how little they knew of the kingdom he came to establish.

Would they learn in due time? It is certain that after he left they would have experience in abundance. But *now*, what of now? Well, he could leave them further instruction. But would they remember? Perhaps if he gave them something so simple and basic that they could not forget, it would form a basis from which they could analyze problems of conduct. And so he said: "A new commandment I give unto you, That ye love one another; as I have loved you, that ye also love one another. By this shall all men know that ye are my disciples, if ye have love one to another" (John 13:34, 35).

In his answer to the lawyer Jesus had given the first and second great commandment as, *Love God*, and *Love neighbor as self*, and had said these were so basic as to form that on which all the law and the prophets could be hung. Now in this upper chamber, he reduced the law to a single command, *Love one another.*

What do you think? If all had this love in heart, would we have need for law? Would there be social evils and sins? How far have *you* gone in developing this great law as a dynamic in your life?

How did this new commandment impress itself upon the disciples? Who knows? It is said that John the Beloved lived to be a very old man. Legend has it that as he lay dying, he raised up and said, "Little children, love one another." It had impressed him deeply. There is no doubt that he had all his life taught it, and as his spirit was about to leave his body he called out what he had come to know was the foundation of all Christian commandments.

● ● ●

The events which followed the upper chamber fellowship were, in the experience of the disciples of Jesus, catastrophic in their effects upon them. He had been betrayed and apprehended in the Garden of Gethsemane. Following this was the trial and condemnation and then the long journey along the Via Dolorosa to the "Place of the Skull"— Golgotha.

How deep and terrible must have been the depression into which the disciples were plunged! They had often seen his power displayed, even to the raising of Lazarus, but before his enemies he seemed utterly helpless. How deep must have been their gloom when he was laid in the rock-sealed tomb. How long the three days must have been, as they hid in seclusion and recounted to one another with abated voices the experiences they had shared with him as they recalled the beauty of his teaching!

Their disappointment and gloom were reflected by the two disciples who, on the road to Emmaus, told the stranger that they hoped it had been Jesus who would have redeemed Israel. For them the death of Jesus had a finality all its own, made more so by the quality of his character. Now, during the time he lay in the tomb, all that had been foremost and uppermost in their minds while they had been with him sank back into the mists of their own doubts.

Then came the glorious news, "He is risen!" They saw him, talked with him again, listened to his instructions once more. Then they saw him ascend into heaven. Who can measure their ecstasy as they comprehended his power as never before and the scope of his teachings? And the promised Comforter, the Great Teacher, the Holy Ghost, the Spirit of God came upon them, and with the endowment thereof and under its impulsion they went out as ambassadors for Christ and witnesses of his resurrection. With great power they preached the Christian gospel, the good news of conquered death and victory over the grave.

One may recall at this juncture the words of the great Augustus Hopkins Strong, the Baptist theologian. He wrote these words sixty years ago in the introduction to his *Systematic Theology:*

We need a new vision of the Saviour like that which Paul saw on the way to Damascus and John saw on the Isle of Patmos, to convince us that Jesus is lifted above space and time, that his existence ante-dated creation, that he conducted the march of Hebrew history, that he was born of a virgin, suffered on the cross, rose from the dead and now lives for ever more, the Lord of the universe, the only God with whom we have to do, our Saviour here, and our Judge hereafter.

It was this kind of conviction that seized the disciples after the Resurrection, lifted them out of and above themselves, and sent them forth radiant with the love and power of God.

Without doubt the apostles were never the same after Calvary and Easter as they were before. Before the Ascension they had Jesus, their leader, with them. To him they could and did turn in every emergency. But when he was gone to the Father, they must determine their own courses, decide their own questions, solve their own problems. To be sure, the promised Comforter was there to guide; but in initiative and action, they must form their own policies, and they grew and expanded in power. They preached as never before, for they taught as men having authority. They rebuked sin, encouraged righteousness, and laid down the principles of life.

Impetuous, emotional Peter, who so often tried the Master, became a power and an anchorage to his brethren. Following Pentecost he stood in boldness, rebuked the Pharisees, denounced sin, and called men to repentance. He told them what they must do to be saved—repent and be baptized.

Some six verses in the second chapter of Acts outline the effect of Peter's words upon those who listened:

Then they that gladly received his [Peter's] word were baptized: and the same day there were added into them about three thousand souls. And they continued steadfastly in the apostles' doctrine and fellowship, and in breaking of bread, and in prayers. And fear came upon every soul: and many wonders and signs were done by the apostles. And all that believed were together and had all things common; and sold their possessions and goods, and parted them to all men, as every man had need. And they, continuing daily with one accord in the temple, and breaking bread from house to house, did eat their meat with gladness and singleness of heart, praising God and having favor with all the people. And the Lord added to the church daily such as should be saved.—Acts 2:41-47.

The three thousand that were baptized were thoroughly converted, not alone with an emotional response to Peter's words, a "getting religion," but they remained steadfast in the breaking of bread and in prayers. Always, in the Christian religion, prayer is associated with daily bread. God intended man to be concerned about his bodily

140

welfare. He intended man to be reasonably comfortable though not to eat beyond his bodily needs; and he therefore blessed the earth that it should bring forth sufficient for all, and even much more. Daily bread bears close relationship to daily prayers.

The fear which came upon every soul was doubtless the "fear of God," that fear of disobeying him. It is a wholesome fear, and prompts to righteousness.

The signs and wonders done by the apostles because of the closeness with which they and the people walked with God hold promise to all peoples answering the call of Christ that obedience brings powers to do even beyond the understanding of man or his ability to explain.

The believers were together. This is the operation of the social law known as "the consciousness of kind." Persons of one mind, one belief, will gather. It is natural and right. Like beliefs in theology merely would not function as strongly as a motive for gathering, as would like-mindedness in social ideals, especially when efforts were being made to put those ideals in realities and work out social problems. That the social factors played prominently in gathering these believers of the teachings of the apostles is evidenced by the statement that they "had all things common."

If we were to stop right there, as some persons do, we might think we would be justified in believing that the apostles taught Communism—that kind of "all things common" according to which all property would belong to the group, whether large or small in number, and that no man would hold property in his own name or in his own right. But the

Reorganized Church of Jesus Christ of Latter Day Saints does not believe that such application of "all things common" was intended by the apostles in their attempt to give social expression to the gospel of Jesus Christ.

The basic law indicated in this early Christian community, was the law of the need. Those who had no need received no part of the surplus thus gathered. And the giving of property to the common treasury for the common good was entirely voluntary. Out of love of God and man came the surplus which those early Christians willingly gave to the common weal. It seems that they observed the law "from each according to his ability, to each according to his need."

This is very far removed from what we today designate as communism. Communism is based upon the denial of the existence of spiritual factors in man's makeup, entails the denial of the existence of God, and designates religion as the opiate of the masses.

What the early Christians enjoyed in this brief but illuminating experiment in social living was far removed from any kind of dictatorship. It was based on the realization given to them that God had indeed broken into their historical experience, and in the gaze upward toward him, they found themselves drawn together in the bonds of fraternity which reached into and controlled every phase in their life.

Someday it must be so with us too.

THE KINGDOM

Someone has said that nothing is so powerful as an idea whose time has come. When Jesus came preaching the kingdom the time had come. A new day had dawned. And, because the time *had* come, the preaching of the Master had revolutionary consequences. He called all alike to an experience brimful of joy. His demeanor did not fit the popular ideas of what a true prophet should say or do.

The earliest pictures of Jesus extant are on the walls of the catacombs in Rome, and were drawn while the Christians were being persecuted. Without exception they depicted Christ as happy—smiling. He called men from the sea, from the field, from the school and the tax gatherer's bench. He invited them to live as he was living—a life of joy. C. S. Lewis tells of his conversion from atheism to Christianity and the title of the book is *Surprised by Joy*. The message of Jesus was one of joy. "Repent," he said, "for the kingdom of heaven is at hand." Or, "Change your lives; something infinitely better is here." He invited men to fellowship with him, and those who responded to the invitation found themselves essaying an incredible happiness.

In response to his teaching many kinds of people came to inquire. There were the religious leaders of the Jews, supercilious, self-satisfied, and questioning. Romans came too—travelers, soldiers, and officials.

Came also the Greeks, always ready to hear and to tell some new thing. Some of those who came sensed in him the promise of a new day, and they stayed and eventually became ambassadors of the new kingdom, anxious to share its ideals.

Ideas are more powerful than armaments. They challenge the existing order with persistent strength. The ideas and ideals which Jesus brought were not entirely new, but what tremendous power they gained when men saw them embodied in his life!

Jesus proclaimed first that Jehovah—King, was also a loving father, concerned with the details of each life. He even marks the sparrows' fall and notes the rising of the sun. He taught men that nothing they could ever do could cause God to cease to care. In all the afflictions of his people he himself was afflicted.

We think such a declaration commonplace and fail to recognize how potent it really is, but the Jewish leaders thought it blasphemy. While many of them wanted to serve Jehovah, they could not bear to see him so belittled as to be concerned about the minute details of their lives. It shocked them to be told that Jesus was the Son of God and that all men might become his sons if only they would obey his teaching. The other day a friend said, "Modern man is confused! He does not really know whom he is supposed to hate." Men can and are taught to hate. Jesus taught them how to love, by calling them into the family of God who was really their loving Father. In his kingdom the most significant figure is the King. The King is also a loving father.

Based upon this revolutionary teaching, the Master proclaimed the law of brotherhood. Men may not love each other because they are commanded to do so. No man can love all men. But all men can love God. In fact they are commanded by Christ to do so. God has made them for himself and when they set their affections upon him with all their might, mind, and strength, they become new creatures. They, by communion with the Father, acquire his loves and hates. They come to see all human beings as the Master saw them, and in such inspirational vision they find the power to love all others.

Jesus did not stop with emphasis upon individual recognition of the love of God. He taught that the only way such love could be expressed was through loving service to neighbor. When man loves God wholeheartedly his whole personality undergoes a tremendous change. The self is healed, and men are set free to love others as they love themselves. No mere changing of the forms of society will do. The social reformation which Jesus aimed at must arise out of individual regeneration.

The kingdom of God is the dominion in which God has sway because, out of their love and gratitude toward him, men give him their joyful allegiance. Then they must not do as they please, but only as God wants them to do, and the nearer they grow to him the more does his will become their will. His will is their peace.

Under the spell of such a spirit all social barriers are cast down. In Christ there is neither male nor female—the greatest of physical distinctions;

neither Jew nor Gentile—the widest gap based on religion. Neither Greek nor barbarian—distinction based on culture; neither rich nor poor—distinction based on wealth. Jew and Gentile, bond and free, Greek and barbarian, rich and poor, as well as male and female all sit down together at the feet of Jesus.

Under the spell of his presence all those different castes saw the promise of new personhood in him which belonged to everyone. They saw the essential brotherhood which bound them together. History has no previous parallel for such an experience as moved the early Christians to share their material possessions in the joy of their newly discovered spiritual equality.

Understanding the ideals of the kingdom is impossible except we shall be divinely enlightened. Jesus recognized this and looked for the great confession which came finally from Peter as Peter had the truth revealed to him. Truly, Jesus is the greatest teacher the world has ever known. But he is more than that. The basic truth upon which the kingdom is built, and separated from which it cannot endure, is the truth that Jesus Christ is the Son of God. This truth can come to us only through the revelation of God.

Individually and collectively we are suffering from spiritual sickness and moral blindness. The blind lead the blind and both fall into the pit. The doctrine of social evolution gives no hope of the divine kingdom. All earlier civilizations have collapsed of their own weight of sin, and signs are not lacking that history will repeat itself.

Only a miracle can save us.

What we need most is not reform but rebirth. Jesus says so, and history confirms his observation. We need to learn how to lose our lives if we are to save them—and indeed save them we cannot in our own strength or by our own devices. Only in the power of reborn lives centered in the love of God will men ever learn to love each other and so discover the ways of peace.

● ● ●

When Jesus followed John in the proclamation of the kingdom he introduced a distinct change of emphasis. Jesus introduced a new note of authority. He extended and expanded John's ministry so much that John began to wonder if all was well. They both proclaimed that the kingdom was at hand, but soon Jesus asserted that it was an accomplished fact. He said that from John onward the kingdom had been preached and all men pressed into it. As the rule or dominion of God was extended in men's lives, just so much was the kingdom established. It is evident that our Lord regarded the nature of the kingdom in a twofold sense. It was first a gift of God and second it was an achievement under God. He told his disciples that in spite of all the trials and difficulties which would surround them, they were not to fear. "It is the Father's good pleasure," he said, "to give you the kingdom." But he also told them that they must seek to build up the kingdom and establish God's righteousness. The kingdom was to come in response to their reception of the gift.

One of the salient features of the ministry of Jesus is his method of using parables as a means of communication. A parable is by dictionary definition a fictitious narrative used to typify moral or spiritual revelations. An old and tried definition runs, "A parable is an earthly story with a heavenly meaning." Perhaps such a description leaves much to be desired, but it is certain that the parables of Jesus were related to and grew out of the reality of the kingdom of God as he saw it. They had a heavenly meaning. But they had an "earthly" meaning, too, in that they were related to reality and to history. Fact and process are to be discerned in all of them. The sower goes forth to sow. The net is cast into the sea. Thus is envisaged in these parables the process we know as the universe. Nature, man, and God are seen in them working together toward the "end" guaranteed in the divine nature and purpose.

Parables, as used by our Lord, indicate the nature of the divine kingdom. They are not told primarily to indicate the times and seasons, although they may do so. The parable of the laborers of the vineyard (Matthew 20:1-5) deals primarily with the justice of God, although it has elements which seem to delineate the various dispensations or "hours" of man's spiritual history. But these historical applications are strictly subordinate to the character of the husbandman which the parable throws into bold relief. The nature of the kingdom arises from the character of the king. Wherever the parables indicate historical suc-

148

cessiveness, they do so to show forth the divine nature, not merely to predict the future.

So, then, parables are symbols of the kingdom. They call men to creative thinking. They both reveal and conceal the truths they emphasize, so that which is revealed may entice such study as to lead men to discover what is concealed. The wise man said, "It is the glory of God to conceal a thing." Divine intelligence is concealed in the parables, and those who search for what is hidden grow in intelligence. Intelligence is the glory of God and is the power by which he works. Man may share that power with him. One of the ways to do this is to search the parables in which are concealed some of the mysteries of the kingdom.

It is not possible to "define" the kingdom any more than one can "define" the Godhead. To "define" is to limit, and no human language is adequate to fully describe these realities. So Jesus called men into adventures in thought and insured their growth as they pondered on his parables. "The kingdom of heaven," he said, "is like..." And it is amazing to consider what a vast range of human life and experience is interpreted by the kingdom motive. It seems as if the whole range of existence is susceptible of such interpretation.

So the kingdom is like a seed which a man took and sowed in his field. The man, of course, is the divine Father, and "his field" is the world. The seed is the promise of the kingdom which the world does not create but which it receives. The kingdom is the kingdom of the Father; it rests on the nature of God. The kingdom must be a gift; it is so distinct from all other kingdoms with which men are familiar that they cannot even describe it.

But the building of the kingdom is an achievement as well as a gift. If Jesus led the way through his divine right in the understanding and acceptance of the gift of God, he led the way just as authoritatively in the achievement of the kingdom. There are various kinds of gifts. Some gifts depend only on the goodwill of the giver and require but little effort on the part of the recipient. Such are gifts of material things. Other gifts are valuable only as the recipient cooperates with the giver. No one can give to men awakened appreciation. This must be won by one's own activity. No one can give a friend a sense of values. This must be self-cultivated. Yet strange as it might seem, the gifts of opportunity, of which the recipient must take advantage through his own activity, are the ones which invariably demand more of the giver than the other gifts which depend merely on his immediate goodwill. Many a father who can secure for his children any material things which might minister to their good finds himself utterly powerless, despite his eagerness, when he desires to win them to an appreciation of the best in life.

The gift of the kingdom of God is a gift of appreciation. God gives himself through revelation to those who persistently seek him, but we must seek continuously, not being satisfied with any fleeting glimpse. Since he is so much greater than

150

man's capacity to understand, and the quality of his greatness defies material measurement, we must develop new standards, new meanings, new measures, new largeness of appreciation. This calls for our own growth.

The establishment of the kingdom of God is an art as well as a science. The artist may be born with certain native genius, but he comes to expertness in the exercise of his gifts only as he develops the power to both see and portray the beauties of life. In the art of heavenly kingdom building the spiritual leaders of men are called to the task of vision and the joy of interpretation.

The greatest artistic achievement is a life made one and whole under the blessings of the kingdom of God. In this achievement all may share through Jesus Christ, our Lord.

● ● ●

The mark of a saint is not perfection, but consecration. A saint is not a man without faults, but a man who has given himself without reserve to God.

It is not by mere machinery that our cities are to be purged, our waste places made glad, and our social life redeemed. The world needs above all else the man who will conceive Christianity as an heroic adventure.

Citizenship in the kingdom of God is no sinecure. It is not an office requiring little or no work, nor is it an ecclesiastical living without the cure of souls. Jesus said, "He that putteth his hand to the plow, and looking back, is not fit for the kingdom of God." One may be born to citizenship in an earthly kingdom or realm and retain his status until he violates the code by the commission of some serious crime. This is not so in the heavenly kingdom, because the King is perpetually at war against evil and entrenched wickedness. None of his subjects can be exempt from taking active part in this warfare. A voluntary and decisive act of righteousness is required of one who enters the kingdom. Continued citizenship requires perpetual activation in righteousness if citizenship is to be maintained.

Sometimes nominal Christians find their way into the church. Occasionally some of these occupy positions of prominence. But these are not actually citizens of the kingdom. It does not take much of a man to be a Christian, but it does take all of him there is.

Before Jesus came, the prophets had pointed out that God welcomes other than Israelites. The Book of Ruth states this clearly. The adventures of Jonah suggest that God loves all men, even those who persecute Israel. Race is no barrier against sin or protection from the consequences of sin. A profession of faith may be welcomed by men, but such a profession coming from men who are insincere or small-souled is not acceptable to God. "Many shall come to me in that day," said Jesus, "and say unto me Lord, Lord."

Jesus established the kingdom and invited all men into it, but he was careful to select only those who were willing to engage in high adventure. He called men to service. He warned them, however, that his service required that they "take up their cross" and follow him. His call to citizenship is like an ever moving fan which sifts the wheat from the chaff. Jesus did not exclude any, but the unworthy excluded themselves. As the author of *Ecce Homo* has written:

He kept them aloof by offering them nothing which they could find attractive. And all those who found Christ's Call attractive were such as were worthy to receive it. Some made up their minds without hesitation. The worldly, the preoccupied turned away with preemptory contempt; a few of rare devotion closed with the Call at once. But the greater number were placed by it in a state of painful suspense and hesitation which lasted a long time. First, to understand distinctly what it was which was proposed to them; next, to make up their minds as to the character of him who made such novel proposals, and advanced pretensions so unbounded; all this cost them much perplexity. But when so much was done, and they had decided favorably to the Prophet and his Theocracy, then came the greater difficulty, that of resolving to embark in an enterprise so unprecedented even at the beck of one whom they acknowledged to hold a divine commission. To break with prejudice and with convention, to enter upon a great and free life, is not done until some doubts have been mastered and some cowardly hesitations silenced.

In the midst of men who were in one state or another of this mental conflict, Christ moved. His words spread around him a perpetual ferment, an ever-seething effervescence. Anxious broodings, waxing or waning convictions, resolutions slowly shaping themselves, a great travail of hearts, went on about him. The Call itself was in his hand as a winnowing fan.

Of this effect produced by his words he was fully conscious. He watched it with constant interest, and of his recorded sayings a large proportion are illustrative descriptions of the different characters. At one time he described the ferment it produced and its gradual diffusion through the community by comparing the kingdom of heaven to leaven which a woman hides in two measures of meal until the whole is leavened. At another time he compares the Call (the Word) to seed sown in different sorts of ground, but bearing a prosperous crop in one sort only. To one class he found it was like a treasure hidden in a field, which not to lose, a man sells all his property and buys the field; to another class it is an invitation which they decline with civil excuses. Thus it shows each man in his genuine character, and, on the whole, those who accept the Call and abide by it are worthy of it.

Jesus believed in the fundamental ability of people. He said they would respond to love and trust and so he taught his followers to love men and to trust them as far as they could. God does this, and men become like God only as they do as God does. Unless he loves and trusts us to the limit, the kingdom can never be. Unless men love each other the kingdom can never be. Jesus was sure men would ultimately behave in this way. So sure was he that he willingly undertook the sacrifice required of him. He knew the day would come when he would find joy in the numbers of men who would thus be redeemed from selfishness.

And so a citizen of the kingdom believes the best about his fellows. Jesus continued to trust Peter after the denial. Peter's denial was not the final word Peter had to say about his Lord. The trust of Jesus triumphed over the wrong.

So we are called to fellowship in the kingdom, a fellowship based upon the revelation of God in Christ and the promise of Christ in every other man. "We know," said John, "that we have passed from death unto life, because we love the brethren."

Such deathless brotherhood moved out into a

cruel world and turned it upside down. The touch of Jesus still has its ancient power. It can turn our selfish hearts into loving ones, too.

• • •

Jesus had keen insight into the motives of men. Oftentimes he confounded his enemies quite easily because of this. When they would entrap him they frequently found themselves without words as he neatly turned the tables on them. But he also saw clearly into the value of what appeared to be the most worthless lives. He was assured that men would eventually respond to the love and goodness of his Father. Yet as he viewed humanity he found it necessary frequently to turn to communion with his Father. Jesus had unmeasured appreciation of God's greatness and this was the secret of his power. Jesus worshiped more than any other man. He knew there was no shadow of evil or darkness in God and responded to that knowledge.

Without doubt, as a lad the glory of the night had beckoned Jesus, and oftentimes he found himself in the hills bathing himself in contemplation of his Father's goodness. Thus he must have watched the sunrise on many occasions. To the tasks of each new day Jesus must have come after such refreshment of soul. He knew the security of communion with God. He knew this as others never knew it.

Peter, for instance, demanded that each day be filled with restless activity. He admonished the church to be diligent always. The Gospel of Mark, based on Peter's preaching, reflects this attitude of ceaseless activity. But Jesus learned to value the moments of quiet contemplation and the strength they gave him as Peter never learned to do. After heavy days of constant teaching, healing, and conflicts with his enemies, Jesus would rather pray than sleep. His strength lay in his worship life.

Bruce Barton, among others, has pointed out that the Western Hemisphere is fertile in material achievements, but the great religions have all come out of the East. The deserts are a symbol of the Infinite. In the West we set great store in *doing*. The East emphasizes *being*. Perhaps it is significant that Jesus lived on the border that divides East and West.

The kingdom of God is a kingdom of worship and adoration. In it men find their souls washed clean, their eyes enlightened, and their determination steeled against the vices and follies of the world. Worship is not impractical. On the contrary, it is quite significant. In worship lies the only source of strength available for those who would assist in the great and marvelous work of kingdom building. In the transfiguration which came to Jesus on the Mount, he found the insight and strength necessary to endure Gethsemane and Golgotha. In the opening scenes of Jesus' life we find wise men coming from afar for the sole purpose of laying their gifts before him and to worship him. Jesus was later to demand from his followers like sacrificial devotion. He knew that worship and service go hand in hand.

There is no doubt that Jesus so identified himself with his cause as to determine that devotion to him could be expressed only in loyalty to the

156

kingdom. Christianity is the worship of Jesus Christ.

Isaiah had seen the vision of the Lord high and lifted up. His experience caused him to say in response to the divine invitation, "Here am I, send me." After his baptism, Jesus went into the wilderness to be with God. The disciples, after the Ascension, went into the quiet solemnity of the Upper Room until they were endowed with power. In seeking the environment and atmosphere in which we can worship, we too can find God.

But worship is not elevating to souls unworthy whose conduct does not reflect social justice and fraternity. Jesus loved the Sabbath day, but he told the Pharisees that its beauty was enhanced through service to the needy. When the Jews were disturbed at thoughts that their temple might be destroyed, Jesus told them that temple gifts were not acceptable if those making the gifts failed to discharge their obligation to needy parents. Men were inclined to measure their devotion by the amount of their offering. But Jesus singled out the widow and her mite as an example to all. And those who brought gifts and did not bring the goodwill and love of their brethren, too, were told to be reconciled to each other and then, and not until then, the gift would be acceptable.

Worship is the quickening of the conscience by the holiness of God. And in the acts of worship we are led to the confession of our sins. We lay our lives alongside his and the comparison which we find there moves us to repentance. For every revelation of the nature of God, there comes to us a winsome desire and the power to become what we see. Worship is the quickening of the conscience by the holiness of God.

Worship is the feeding of the mind or the edification of the soul by the truth of God. And this is done as we listen to his word, as we read it or recite it, as it is preached from the pulpit, or as we are taught the divine word through the various gifts and offices of the church; or when we listen to the authentic voice of the Spirit speaking in the outward gifts of the gospel or, more especially, when we have learned to listen in silence to the inner voice which calls us forward, and which lifts us up and cheers us, forgives our sins and condemns us in our sins, and offers to us continually the renewal and the benediction of a fresh start. Worship is the feeding of the soul and the mind, the edification of the man by the truth of God.

Worship is the gathering of all the facets of our nature—our conscience, our minds, our imaginations, our hearts, and our wills—into one attitude of adoration, which is the most selfless emotion of which man is capable, the spirit of awe that takes your breath away and lifts you out of yourself. You are caught up in a moment of rapture, in a moment eternal, as you worship before the throne of God. Your very nerve cells cry out for the living God. You know that your sin and transgression have left their record within your body, and that record must be erased—and will be under the providence and the cleansing power of the love of God. And you say, "We give thanks unto thee for thy great glory."

The strength of the kingdom lies in its fidelity to the nature of God. And his nature is mediated to men as they truly worship him.

• • •

Jesus had no easy time. In his efforts to promote his kingdom he was continuously thwarted by the ambitions of his fellows. On one occasion a rich young man, full of promise, turned away sorrowing because his love of money kept him from the kingdom. The businessmen surrounding the Master were too busy making money to make the decision for righteousness. Even the Temple courts were the scene of sordid money-grubbing, promoted and concurred in by the priests.

Christ was not opposed to riches. He fraternized with rich as well as poor. But he knew the temptations which came to those who had money and the power it brings. In those days great wealth was not often obtained except by deceit and trickery, and where men made profit their chief motive in life self-judgment was very difficult. Men have always been extremely clever at excusing their own weaknesses, and wealth has a way of blinding the eye to the sufferings of others. The story of the rich man and Lazarus illustrates this clearly.

Yet Jesus knew the actual severity of poverty. The great curse of poverty is not alone lack of material resources. It is rather the restrictions of personality through denial of nourishment and cultural opportunity. Poverty has a way of engendering resentment and bitterness with consequent sickness of soul.

There is a great distinction to be made between business in the kingdom of God and the economics of the kingdoms of this world. At the beginning of his work Jesus said that a man should not live by bread alone. He did not deny that men needed bread. His own life illustrated this. When a man, disgruntled because he had received an unequal share of an inheritance, came to the Master, he was reminded that a man's life did not consist in the abundance of the things that he possessed. Many times things have a way of possessing a man. The rich man who built bigger barns so he could "take life easy" Jesus called a fool. The widow who gave her all gave more than those who gave merely out of their surplus. In her gift was the full devotion of her heart.

The scribes and Pharisees on the other hand loved the pleasant attractiveness of affluence. The rich were their friends, regardless of how the riches were obtained or how callous toward the poor was the attitude of those who had them. To the scribes, wealth and social position became the same as inward goodness. They were lovers of money and scoffed at Jesus who passed up so many chances for graft. Being covetous they robbed the widows and tried to cover their extortions with prayer.

Jesus was not primarily interested in social and economic theory. He came to bring men new life. But he understood clearly the difference between acquisitiveness and service and service in deed, as so much is today, with an acquisitive motive. He clearly told his followers they must choose between them. "No man," he said, "can serve two masters." Some chose mammon. Others pointed to existing economic conditions and sought to justify themselves. These people Jesus invited into his kingdom and said that whoso sought his kingdom first would find all things else (that is all things necessary to the finding of the kingdom) added unto them. Jesus meant by this that with the elimination of lust and avarice and greed, power to deal justly and equally would be granted to men. This would result in the equitable distribution of the goods of life.

Jesus had no conflict with riches as such. "Behold I have made the earth rich," he says in modern revelation, "and behold, there is enough for all and to spare." The danger of power lies in its misuse. "All power corrupts," said Lord Ackon, "and absolute power corrupts absolutely." The power of wealth is easily misused since there are no effective safeguards against abuse. But any man of power who uses his gifts for private and personal gain rather than for the general good of mankind destroys his own best self. You cannot serve God and mammon. You must choose between them, between the use of your wealth—money, gifts, or talents—for the good of mankind or for its use for selfish purposes. The choice is really between the dominion of God in your life and the dominion of self.

Jesus knew the meaning of industry. At the base

of the community is the mass of manual and mental labor. Jesus had shared this. He had mixed with the small men of his community, the farmers, the fishermen, and the manual laborers. He had, with them, been shouldered away from the chief seats at the feasts. He knew the widow who had hunted for the piece of money she had lost. He knew the friendship of uncorrupted rich men like Nicodemus and Joseph of Arimathea. He knew the heartwarming sharing of Mary and Martha and Lazarus. He knew by his many contacts with rich and with poor that God measures men by what they do in relation to their opportunities.

In the kingdom of this world, currency is used to purchase satisfaction of material wants. The currency of the kingdom of God is used solely to satisfy human needs and in building and enriching personality. The law of mammon is greed. The law of God is love. As men may determine either may banish the other, but the two cannot work together.

The accumulation of money robs itself. Rich men, even today, are in bondage in many ways. They are the objects of envy and jealousy on the part of many who would rob them. The treasures of the kingdom are, on the other hand, eternally secure. No one can be robbed of these.

It is nearly two thousand years since Jesus called us to his new standard of values. Many who today give him lip service still deny him and mock him by their actions. They still say in their hearts that he is an impractical dreamer. But Christian communities everywhere are beginning to demand

162

that industry shall conform to Jesus' principle of reverence for personality. Both in the production and distribution of goods and services the Christian standard of righteousness must unceasingly prevail.

• • •

In the teaching and work of Jesus Christ there are certain fundamental principles, which if accepted, not only condemn much in the present organization of society, but show the way of regeneration. In the light of the principles of Christianity, the construction of society, the conduct of industry, the upbringing of children, and in fact all human relationships must be tested.

One of the obvious laws which Jesus kept inviolate was the law governing the Sabbath day. His observance was part of his upbringing. It is so commonplace that we today tend to overlook it. Jesus complied with the divine law given through Moses and completely fulfilled its requirements. He was accused of Sabbath breaking by his enemies, but upon investigation, their accusations proved groundless. His criteria was, "Is it lawful to do good on the Sabbath day?" He said the Sabbath was made for man and not man for the Sabbath. Evidently it was, for him, the day set apart especially for divine worship. Our generation misses much in its violation of Sabbath observance. The quiet strength and peace that comes from worship of the heavenly King cannot be given to a people feverishly bent upon pleasure.

Jesus was taught in his home at his mother's knee. What a tremendous responsibility was laid upon her! Yet it was the law in Israel that all children should be taught. The most amazing fact in history is the existence of the Jews, whose national life has persisted through the ages. They have been persecuted, hated, driven about. For generations they had no country to call their own, no rulers, no written constitution, and yet they have preserved their national characteristics. This has been accomplished through the system of education fostered among them. This command to teach their children was given through Moses, and Jesus honored and supported it. He commanded the little children to come to him and told his disciples to forbid them not. In the kingdom of God those who fail to teach their children light and truth are condemned.

The Mosaic law demanded of the people a strict observance of the laws governing the disposing of their finances. Tithes and offerings were expected, and the scribes and Pharisees were meticulous in their observance of the law and its letter. But Jesus asked more. He taught that sacrifice lay at the heart of the kingdom way of life and commended the widow who gave all because she loved the kingdom.

It is not enough to observe the letter of the law. Unless our love for the kingdom and its ways goes beyond conventional giving we never discover the enrichment of personality which the spirit of sacrifice can make possible. Love, which is the very spirit of the kingdom of God, has only one instrument by which its purposes can be achieved, and that is sacrifice. Sacrifice is a law of the kingdom. As the Psalmist has said, speaking of the end of history, "Gather my saints together unto me, those that have made a covenant with me by sacrifice."

Life in the kingdom is disciplined. It is disciplined because it is guided by a vision of its task. Where there is no vision, we are told, the people perish. They perish because they lack restraint. There is no greater example of a disciplined life than that of Jesus. He permitted nothing extraneous to his life's purpose to engage his powers. Always, what he did was consistent with his one aim in life, to do his Father's will. "I do always those things," he said, "which please the Father." Similarly those who are committed to the unfinished tasks he left them to do cannot afford to waste their powers in frivolity. Paul realized this and wrote, "This one thing I do, forgetting those things which are past I reach forward. . . ."

What the kingdom offers to us is a vision of a new humanity. Anyone who really sees Jesus sees his own better self and willingly undertakes those disciplines which will help him achieve what he sees. The followers of the Master always have found the power, in his name, to put lust behind them and persist within themselves until Christ's righteousness prevails in them. Men under God are men under discipline. They cease to do evil by learning to do well.

The whole law of the kingdom is caught up in the word *stewardship*. Those who come to know the love of God realize that all they are and all they have is a trust, bestowed upon them by the Father. Their use of what they are and of what they have determines their character and their eternal destiny. The law of stewardship is the only way man can express his love for God and his fellows. With Jesus, God was the most significant fact of history. Along with this, the love of God toward men and their consequent value saturated all he did. The sense of the nature of God became the measure by which Jesus evaluated all things.

This is the secret of his insight. It was because Jesus saw in sin the means by which men were stultified that he hated sin so passionately. How much a man hates sin is in direct proportion to his love for God. Jesus had complete fellowship with his Father and sought parallel fellowship with men—not with men as they were but as he saw they might become. He made no compromise with worldliness, and neither should we.

Jesus was sure that because God was God, and the kind of Being he was, all things must eventually make for man's eternal welfare. He knew that evil must inevitably pass away and give place to the kingdom of beauty, truth, and goodness. He knew that the kingdoms of this world will eventually be replaced by the kingdom of God. So, confident in such knowledge, he moved with certainty and poise to the time and place where the kingdom of love poured itself out in utter sacrifice to win the souls of men.

● ● ●

Jesus had a wide circle of friends. His range of interest in his fellows was unlimited. His appreciation of men included both friend and foe. Other world teachers have addressed themselves to mature minds and totally ignored little children; Jesus appealed to children most strongly. Always they came to him without fear of his rebuke. With shepherds, farmers, and fishermen, Jesus was friendly. He knew the religious leaders of the community. With Roman soldiers and civil officers he had always been familiar. Jesus had a wide variety of contacts with his fellows. But, of itself, this does not fully explain the universal quality of his interest in people nor the worldwide scope of his teachings. The reason lies deeper. It is found not primarily in Christ's interest in men but in God. His unique relationship with his Father determined his outlook on men.

We do not know all that Jesus meant when he said God was a Father. It meant more than just "Creator" and certainly included and went far beyond what we mean when we think of fatherhood at its best. We do know a good father loves all his children, good and bad, and he seeks their welfare at any cost to himself. "God so loved the world that he gave his only begotten Son"; and the Son, in turn, so loved that he gave himself for our redemption and willingly identified himself with his Father's purpose.

His promises were to "all," to "everyone," to "whosoever" and to those in the uttermost parts of the earth. His favorite term used in describing himself was "the Son of Man"—signifying his complete identity with mankind as a whole.

The story of the one lost sheep and the parable of the prodigal son reflect the missionary spirit of the Master. Christ invited the weary: "Come unto me, all ye that labor and are heavy laden." He invited those who were starved of soul, the lost, and the "other sheep" not of Judah's fold to share with him in the loving tasks of the kingdom.

When Christ's work with and among the Jews brought him in contact with people of alien races, his gracious ministry went freely to them too. There was a Samaritan woman to whom he revealed his Messiahship; the Roman centurion whose faith healed his servant; the Canaanitish woman whose daughter was healed. Even in his death his glory reached out and touched a Roman soldier who acknowledged Christ's divinity at the very time his own disciples had forsaken him. He came to save the world, as he said; and as he contemplated the completion of his mission he exclaimed, "I, if I be lifted up, will draw all men unto me." Since then it has been so. So, when the great commission was given to the disciples, he said, "Go ye into all the world, and preach the gospel to every creature."

The kingdom of God is for all: "Whosoever will may come and drink of the waters of life freely." We have understood the great commission of Jesus, his command to go into all the world, mainly or chiefly in a geographical context. But why is it not also related to every phase of life? Why is it not intensive as well as extensive? Should the ambassadors of the kingdom not go into politics as well as into Bolivia? Into economics as well as Equador? Into social life as well as into Siberia? Into education and medicine too? In fact, the gospel of the kingdom creates concern for all men, every-where, and it creates concern in all that men do. The purpose of the kingdom is to penetrate the whole of common life, causing Christ to confront men in each and every phase of life.

It has been observed many times that what we *see* is dependent upon what we *seek*. Point of view is all important as we delve into the story of Jesus. The events of his life are so saturated with light and truth that to understand them fully they must be studied from many angles of vision. No viewpoint is more revealing than the missionary viewpoint. Only those who are moved by a passion for the souls of men can really understand why Jesus came to earth. He envisioned a redeemed humanity, many of whom should come from the East and from the West and from the North and the South and should sit down in the kingdom of God.

The kingdom is passionately missionary. God seeks all men to share with him and each other and as stewards over the divine ideal and resources. Those who were nearest Jesus were all missionaries.

If a man desires the continued indwelling of Christ's Spirit he may have it if he is willing to endeavor to take the gospel to others. The strength of God's kingdom is in its power to proselyte. Missions perpetuate the church.

The King cannot be content as long as there is one soul outside his realm. So much do men mean to him that he gave himself to win them to him.

Those who are won to him become like him as they live with him in worship. So they, too, evidence the same concern for others that God has for them, and endeavor for others what Christ has done for them.

It has been said that the Bible is the story of man's search after God, but this is hardly true. The reverse is true. It is the story of God's search after man. The first question ever asked of man by his Creator was, "Where art thou?" Man has hidden himself away from God in this materialistic age where the cardinal sin is to call sin by another name. And still, as of old, God seeks man because he loves him. The King, whose nature is love, gives that nature to his kingdom, and so the citizens of that kingdom, as does their King, give themselves to seek and save that which is lost.

● ● ●

The concern of good men has always made itself felt, especially in times of crisis. One such good man was Charles Gore, the English saint and scholar. He wrote in 1921 following the first World War:

Like others, as I view the world and the church at the present day, I cannot feel hopeful about the immediate prospect. The prophets and experience alike convince me that there can be no real social recovery except through a general return to God. And of such a return I see no signs. God has smitten, but in general we have not sought Him. Thus, taught by the prophets, I am ready to anticipate scathing judgements. But the prophets also teach us to hold with unquenchable faith to the divine purpose of progress, through all the catastrophes and judgements which widespread apostasy from God brings with it.

His anticipation of scathing judgments has since been fully justified. We have sustained a great economic depression, another world war, Korea and Viet Nam, and the end of this no man can foresee. In addition, social upheaval and racial conflict is our portion here in the United States. The "domestic tranquillity" which the founding fathers sought to ensure for us is no accident, and cannot be guaranteed except through obedience to the law of man's being. Peace is no happenstance. It is the result of obedience to law. Social justice, based on the concept that each man counts for one, and for no more than one, must play its full part in any peaceful society.

This is objectified in our Lord's summary of life in our times. He said, "Because iniquity shall abound, the love of man shall wax cold." Who can deny that today the texture of fraternity is very thin indeed. The word *iniquity* is derived from a Latin source, and at root means "injustice, inequality, unfairness." Envy and jealousy are engendered where inequality abounds. Men are created to be free and equal; where freedom or equality is violated social disharmony and conflict is the result. Perhaps later we shall have more to say on the meaning of equality. Now we wish to say something more about divine judgment.

There is no doubt but that Jesus viewed human conduct as always under divine judgment. Every philosopher worthy of the name has stressed the fact that no one can escape the consequences of his actions. Emerson affirmed the doctrine most clearly when he said, "What a man does, that he has." All of us are what we are as a result of the operation of the principle of judgment, and there is none to escape. Although the results of such judgment are not always immediately apparent, they are nevertheless sure.

But divine judgment on men, and on nations, is no capricious affair. The divine law operates always and everywhere with complete impartiality. We reap what we sow. We are what we do. Judgment is utterly inevitable, but it is not vindictive. The divine Father loves his children and all whom he has created are beneficiaries of his concern and his care. Because God does love us, he can tolerate no favorites. He cannot take "time off," so to speak, from any one of us for any other. He must punish transgression because his love demands that he be satisfied with nothing but the best of which each is capable. The "scathing judgments" to which reference has been made are simply his means of awakening within each of us, and within mankind generally, the sense that law has been broken. Really, judgment is an expression of his kindness which seeks to plant the flag of love within the citadel of the rebellious spirit. Judgment is not vindictive; it is remedial. The pain that accompanies disease in the physical body is an indication that the body is malfunctioning, and constitutes an invitation to apply remedial measures. The human body is governed by law, and when the law is adhered to the body is preserved.

This is true also in a social sense. Joy, peace,

happiness, and beauty—all the values the human spirit longs for and has a right to—are governed and preserved by law. The law was revealed in its fullness by Christ. When misery, war, and unhappiness are experienced, his law has been broken. "Every transgression receives a just recompense of reward," said Paul. Social conflict and dislocation is a result of broken law—the law of love. This is not to say that anyone is particularly guilty. We are not speaking of guilt or trying to affix "blame." We are simply pointing out that judgment is a result of broken law, and while no particular one of us may be guilty all of us are at fault. And the fault lies deep in our unwillingness to do unto others as we would they should do to us. Such social consciousness is all too rare, but if our world is to be spared further "scathing judgments" this law must be obeyed. Men must learn to love each other. The law of love must be taught.

Can it be done? Will ever there be a race of men who seek first the interest of neighbor and subordinate their own interests to that of others? In view of the tendency of bias toward evil which appears in every one of us, it seems doubtful that ideal conditions will ever prevail on the earth.

Not even the most refined and most highly developed religious character can live the Christian religion on his own, or by himself. He must interact with others to develop his character. It takes more than one man and God to live the Christian religion. Each man must be neighbor to all others, and demonstrate his love for God in service to his brother. Our hope and prayer should ever be and our work directed so that this conception of the Christian religion may expand in ever widening circles. Let it encompass all mankind so that wars may cease and the kingdom of God come as a welcome gift and not as a scathing judgment to the condemnation of the race.

CHRISTIAN LIFE

What should Christians stand for in the secular world? How should they think and react toward those whose whole lives are spent thinking about the merely temporal things and who believe only in what they can experience through the five senses?

Secularism is that tendency, especially dominant in our time, which seeks the fulfillment of man's whole nature in his earthly existence. This tendency, although not formally organized into any social community, is nevertheless prominent everywhere. It even infects many who are regular churchgoers. But it is not Christian in any sense of the word. Christianity claims authentic tidings of invisible things. It claims that this temporal world has been invaded by a spiritual realm, which has changed its character and meaning. What must the Christian stand for in the secular world?

First he must stand for God, who has spoken. A vague theism is absolutely futile. H. G. Wells spoke of God as an invisible King, who was another name for collectivized man. Some scientists speak of him as a "Great Thinker" who designed the universe but has nothing in common with our hopes and wishes, our longings, disappointments, and frustrations. When Christians talk about God, they mean the person who was revealed in Jesus

Christ. This God is the Creator and Sustainer of all that is, who, for us men and our salvation, was made manifest in the meridian of time, and who is to come again to judge the living and the dead. Vague theism is not enough. The Christian must stand for the God whom Jesus revealed.

From *Sense, Nonsense and Christianity*, by Hugo Meynell, comes the following:

That Jesus Christ is true God and true man entails that our ultimate fate is determined by our relationship to him; that all of our other relationships in this world and the next, and everything that can possibly happen to us, are in comparison of no importance whatever.

It is not easy to maintain one's integrity and steadfastness in the world in which we live today. We are deluged with mass suggestions designed with the utmost skill and at great expense by those who have something to sell. And what are these mass suggestions based on? They are based on the assumption that the only ends in life worth pursuing are money, social prestige, positions of influence, and "making it" with the opposite sex. They appeal to covetousness, pride, the desire for power, ambition, and lust. Look at the advertisements on billboard and in newspaper and ask yourself to which of your impulses they are addressed. The late William George Peck said, "If I'm the sort of being that the man who designed those advertisements thinks I am, then I'm not the sort of being the Gospel thinks I am."

If we are to maintain the primacy of God in our minds, both subconsciously and consciously, then we must always be questioning the scale of values which underlies our modern secular society, not only

176

as it is revealed in the advertisements but also that which comes to us through newspapers, books, films, and television. In this regard the advice of Paul is apropos:

Finally, brethren, whatsoever things are true, whatsoever things are honest, whatsoever things are just, whatsoever things are pure, whatsoever things are lovely, whatsoever things are of good report; if there be any virtue, and if there be any praise, think on these things.

And he would remind us to "let this mind be in you that was in Christ Jesus."

These scriptural injunctions were reinforced in modern revelation when the church was admonished to "let the solemnities of eternity rest upon your minds" and "practice virtue and holiness before me continually." And when the solemn school for the ministry was organized, the following advice came to the elders:

If your eye be single to my glory, your whole bodies shall be filled with light and there shall be no darkness in you, and that body which is filled with light comprehendeth all things. Therefore sanctify yourselves that your minds become single to God, and the day will come that you shall see him: for he will unveil his face to you, and it shall be in his own time, and in his own way, and according to his will.... Prepare yourselves, purify your hearts, and cleanse your hands and your feet before me, that I may make you clean; that I may testify to your Father, and your God and my God, that you are clean from the blood of this wicked generation, that I may fulfill this promise, this great and last promise which I have made unto you when I will.

Although this was given to a past generation and in other conditions than those which prevail today, yet it expresses valid principles. Those who are careless about their conduct cannot grow in spiritual and mental power. Always achievement waits on discipline. The freedom to behold the glory of God comes only after a long period of arduous mental and spiritual exercise, and a constant turning and returning of the mind to dwell on those things which have been revealed in the divine Word.

No one can really appreciate a great painting by taking an occasional peek at it. Nor can he enjoy a great symphony by listening at odd intervals to snatches from it. To enjoy a great painting one must gaze and gaze until he is gripped by its beauty and receives its message. If he would really understand a great piece of music he must bathe his soul in the sweet concourses of sound time and time again. Similarly, if Christians would be free from the thralldom of this secular age, and be enabled to fix themselves on the glory and the love of God, they must worship regularly every day, and day after day. The time when we Christians most need to pray is when we feel least like praying.

The real problems of the Christian life usually come where people do not look for them. They start immediately when we wake up each morning. All the problems of the day come crowding in and the demands which are to be made upon time and energy are evaluated, and they rush at us like wild animals. Then the very first thing that is required of a Christian is that he push them all back where they belong and try deliberately to take another point of view, recognizing that what is important for each and every day is not what he wants primarily, but what God wants of him.

It is not easy to do this, but it is very rewarding.

Gradually, as this habit of daily worship is formed and fixed so that the Good Spirit will invade the soul and influence all we do, a larger, stronger, quieter and fuller life will flow into the soul. Christians must stand for God in the secular world, and prayer is a means to such posture.

● ● ●

It is a secular world in which we live. This means that the general outlook is governed by the fact that mankind as a whole tends to see in the temporal things of life their whole means and ends of existence. Against this point of view Christians must stand for God and his revelation of himself in history. To assert that there is and can be no higher life than the one we know in this temporal sphere is, we believe, not true to the facts. Christianity asserts that this world was invaded by a spiritual world which is above and beyond it, and from which alone it draws its significance and meaning.

Men were not born to be butchers and bakers and candlestick makers. They were born to be the sons of God. The first great commandment is that we love God with all our being, and the second, so "like unto it" that it cannot be distinguished from the first, is that we love our neighbor as ourselves.

How do we stand before God in actual fact? If Jesus is to be believed, we each count for one and no more than one. The divine perfection is seen in the fact that he sends his rain on the just and the unjust, and his sunshine on the good and the evil. His nature is a righteousness which is perfect love; and so he purposes the establishment of justice in all spheres of life—personal, social, cultural, economic, political, and international. A decision for God involves on the part of Christians a sharp break from the secularist tendencies of our time which seek the whole fulfillment of man's life in his earthly existence.

Man is free to rebel, and has done so, in spite of the marvels of science and human wisdom, and what they have done in controlling his own destiny. But man cannot escape the divine sovereignty. To deviate from the divine law is to incur disaster, and such disaster comes by the operation of what scientists call "natural law." Natural law operates at the divine behest and the disasters which come upon people of wickedness are his judgments set in the natural course in order to safeguard the creation. God has laid on man the duty of decision, and some Christians seek to evade responsibility by casting it back upon him, and so try to escape.

Faith in God is never an escape from life or its judgments. Nor is faith a substitute for hard-headed scientific thought. Our intellectual faculties are God's gift to us, for his glory is intelligence. The Christian faith must, if it is to survive and destroy the subtle influence of Marxism and secular humanism, give men a living, vital content for their faith. These influences have some element of truth in them, but this element of truth can be absorbed by an articulate and intelligent Christian faith. Karl Marx discovered nothing about men and history that was not already known by the Lord Jesus, and modern secularism may not be as new as many of its devotees seem to think.

No enlightened Christian today would question the right of men of science to question and question again and again that which is capable of being investigated. The complex problems of our present society cannot be resolved without a continuous expansion of scientific knowledge especially in the field of social science. But we must not make the mistake of substituting the scientific approach to reality for the Christian approach. The two are not incompatible, it is true, but we make the mistake today of thinking that the scientific attitude is the only sane approach to reality. We must be thankful for the scientists and must make the fullest use of them, but their approach is only one, and it is not the most fundamental, nor is it the most important approach.

The scientist sits in his ivory tower and asks questions and expects answers. He is king, and demands and receives the homage due a king. But is this the way life really is? No. Let the scientist meet another person who, like himself, is king in his own world, and then the situation is quite different. In his encounter with another person or group the scientist is no longer free to ask what he will and to order things as he pleases. Questions may be asked of him which require an answer. He is no longer the sole judge but is himself subject to judgment. And there is a profound difference in these two approaches to reality. They are not interchangeable, and all of us are tempted at times to bring the relations between ourselves and others into the framework of the self-centered view.

We can learn a lot about people by studying them medically, psychologically, or sociologically. But thus we never really meet them, and it is in the meeting of people that real life consists. Science is fundamentally individualistic while the interplay of life is in the continuous adjustment one man makes to another and the adjustment achieved between groups.

If all of us recognized this fundamental truth, it would create a quite different spiritual and intellectual climate in which to do business. Men can live in peace if only they recognize they do not know it all and each group renounces the claim to have the final say-so. Our highest act of worship is never a "flight into the alone" but a social meal, a holy communion. Among other doctrines, the truth about God is that he designs all to become his sons and daughters, and the truth about our neighbor which is of paramount importance is that he was designed so to become.

We must cease to think alone of our relation to God, or only about our relationship with neighbor. We must think of both at the same time. Dr. Frederick M. Smith made an appeal for a new social consciousness in these words:

Religion in the Christian sense is comprised of service—service to those in need, service to others—altruism. And this makes religion much more than meditation, prayer, and observance of ceremonies. It is meditation become dynamic, it is prayer plus the desire to do, it is ceremony followed by action. It is meditation, prayer, and ceremony vitalized and sanctified by beneficent action in service to others.

To follow Jesus as believer, disciple, and servant, man must hold all his possessions, his life, his conduct, his attitude, and his money at the service of God, ready to utilize all in the service of his fellow man, as full duty to Deity.

Any social order based on selfishness is fundamentally wrong. Who will deny that today the appeal for endeavor is to selfishness? In the school, on the street, in the bank, from the rostrum, in union headquarters, from the pulpit, in the factory, the appeal is largely, if not entirely, to the selfish instinct. Individuals are urged to endeavor, but for reward. Service is urged, but in the line yielding the largest returns to the individual. Professions are chosen for the prospective return, and excellence therein is striven for because larger tolls can be collected, and the struggle is to amass a competency or more, for the power brought or for the chance for early retirement with security from worry or work. Our industry is based on the reward to self and on fear. Men toil in fear of old age and insecurity. What a travesty on the Christian religion! A society ostensibly Christian whose industrial impulsion is fear, or the appeal to self, when Christianity is based on love—love of God and neighbor.

As William Temple has said:

A decision for sociality as the basic truth of human existence would create an outlook and temper so different from that which has been dominant in the modern era now drawing to its close as to create a new epoch in human history.

Such decision will only come as mankind responds to the teaching of the meek and lowly Nazarene.

● ● ●

Christians believe that the most important aspect of man's life here, and hereafter, is his relation to God and to his fellowman. While this is true, man's life is also set in an order of nature which is God's ordinance. So that man has a fundamental duty to reverence the natural order recognizing that God made it. It is a creature, not a thing.

Today there is no effective Christian witness in relation to the temporal order. It is exploited ruthlessly so that it might gratify our whims and desires. Of course there are national parks and game preserves, but these are a witness to man's rapacity and the result of laws designed to set limits to it. If effective witness in relation to the temporal order is to be forthcoming, a fundamental change of outlook is required by Christians in regard to it.

We tend to exploit the physical world. We are part animal and so a part of nature, dependent and interdependent upon the temporal order. We must reverence its economy. It is true we are called to have dominion over all the works of God's hands. But we must do so as senior partners, not as superior beings who are entitled by nature to extract from it that which merely gratifies our desires.

The notion that the earth has a soul-life of its own has long been a teaching of Latter Day Saints. In this connection the following quotation by Dr. L. P. Jacks is of decisive interest. In his book, *A Living Universe*, written many years ago, he writes:

There are in the last resort only two doctrines possible as to the nature of the universe—one holding it to be dead, lifeless, a mechanism going by a kind of clockwork, and the other holding it to be essentially alive—and that not as a cabbage is alive, but as we are, conscious of itself as a unitary whole, and knowing what it is about. This is the doctrine which I find myself forced to accept as by far the better alternative of the two. The sayings of the gospel—"God is not a God of the dead but of the living"—I take as covering everything in space and time, all that the astronomers tell us that is going on in the unimaginable depths of space, all that the historians can tell us of what has gone on in the unimaginable depths of time.

All is alive, and it is one life, frankly an immortal life, that animates the whole.... If, then, there is anything in which I am one with that universe, anything in which I am the sharer in its life, then, too, I become a sharer in its immortality. Life and immortality, not death and mechanism, are the key-words of the real universe, and so far as you and I are true sons of the universe, so far as we reproduce its nature in ourselves, life and immortality are the key-words to our reality, also....

When the universe is thought of in this manner (as living in itself)—and it is only the accident of our times and the peculiar mental habits and stock notions we have developed, which make it difficult for us so to think of it—when the universe is thought of in this manner, it ceases to be the mere scene or theatre on which our life is transacted—which is all a dead universe can ever amount to. It becomes essentially a Companion, a living Companion—no new idea, but one which was perfectly familiar to the Stoics and may be found running through all the writings of Marcus Aurelius. That being so, there is now room for raising the question whether you and your Great Companion are not fellow-workers, out for the same thing, whether your purpose and your business are not one with the purpose and business on which the Soul of the World is also intent.

All this is beautifully said. And it is the Christian viewpoint. In this secular world Christians must stand for the proposition that man is grounded in nature.

It is not only in physical nature that man's life is rooted; he shares a common humanity, which is also part of nature. There is a grave error characteristic of the times in which we live. It is that we place too exclusive an emphasis on politics as a means of solving social problems to the exclusion of other equally important spheres of human life and activity. Man is not ruled alone by his reason and his conscious aims, and therefore his ills cannot be cured alone by adopting the right will and the proper aims. Our life here is inextricably interwined with natural associations of family, livelihood, tradition, and culture. When, for instance, family ties are disrupted and broken, the whole life of society is thereby enfeebled. There are human considerations which precede politics, although recognition of this fact should not be made an excuse for evading political decisions. Political decisions of far-reaching consequence have to be made, and the way they are made will have a direct bearing on our social life.

There are spheres of human life which need to be enlivened and made healthy again and in turn these will affect political sanity and vigor. Until this secular age began at the end of World War I, most of the natural forms of association and most of the cultural patterns were sponsored, to a great extent, under Christian influences. Now new ideas of the nature of reality have taken the place of the old ones. Man's emotional life is being fashioned under entirely new rituals, and even where the aims are nominally Christian the souls of men are often molded by alien influences. It seems almost as if the real crisis we face is not a moral one but a cultural crisis. And the remedy is not to be found in most of what the church is doing today—that is, in insisting on ideals and in bolstering the will to follow them.

Moral advice is important where it is not divorced from social structure. It is society that educates and molds the youth. Where exhortation and suggestion are at variance, exhortation always loses and suggestion always wins. As Dr. McDowell used to say, "What you *are* speaks so loudly that I cannot hear what you say."

Many educators, among them Dr. Joseph Kinmont Hart, have pointed out that the chief instrument of education is the community itself. All of us are subject to a massive assault upon our spiritual life, from the streets, from the schools, from the mass media of communication. Not all these agencies are harmful, but enough of them are that they tend to determine the kind of people we are. If the Christian witness is to be more effective, Christians must recognize that community is the chief means of molding men, and human behavior is determined as much if not more by subconscious egotisms, interests, and deceptions imposed by nature and man's place in history as by his cultural patterns. This is illustrated by an experience of a friend of mine who remonstrated with her little grandson for watching so many bloodthirsty movies on television. "Jimmy," she said, "you don't want to watch all those killings." "But, Grandma," he rejoined, "I love killings."

The recognition that man is grounded in nature will lead those of us who are committed to Jesus Christ to create such environments in our homes as shall testify of him. The pictures on the walls, the music we hear, the plays we watch, and the magazines we read should all be carefully screened in order that the total home environment shall testify of the Lord Jesus.

● ● ●

It is perfectly natural for men to be self-centered. It is supernatural for them to be wholly altruistic so that they and their means are dedicated to the welfare of others. Yet it is only through the elimination of self-centeredness that we can hope to assuage the ills of our world. Why is it natural for men to be self-centered?

When we were created, we were created for our heavenly Father; we do not belong to ourselves. We have no primary rights over our own lives. He has rights in our existence which belong to no other person. This is the meaning of the phrase in the Ten Commandments, "Thou shalt have no other gods before me." We are made in the image of God. Even our physical frame reflects his divine being. We are conscious of being selves, and self-consciousness and the consciousness of sin are part of being human.

We come into this world and it lies around us; we imagine that we are the center of it, not only physically, which of course is true for each of us, but morally and spiritually. As we grow up, we become conscious of existence. Our first consciousness is not of self but of relationship between parent and child. We grow up in an Eden of peace and delight. At first the baby does not know that it has been separated from its parent body. The first relationship is one of utter dependence. Some things hurt us, some things please us. Things that please us we hope will happen again, and we call them good. But things that hurt us we hope will not happen again. We call them bad. We welcome and hope for the recurrence of the things that please us, but the things that displease us we turn away from.

So, as we grow up, we become the center and the standard of reference of our own moral world. The value judgments we form are based upon the way life affects us. We have a standard of values which we borrow from our past experience. We begin our lives in a truth and a lie. It is true that we are the center of the universe physically, but it is not true that we are the center of the universe morally. God is.

As we recognize that we are the center of the universe physically, so morally we commit the error of thinking that our standard of values is final, our judgments upon life are ultimate. "And every man walketh in his own way, and after the image of his own god." We were doing this before we were conscious that we were doing it, and we are not *guilty* as a result. But we are certainly in a position which brings dismay and a disruption of life to us and to all others who are around us unless it is corrected.

In recent years there has been in certain circles a distinct awakening of social consciousness, and we might begin to hope that the crest of the wave of selfishness which has swept over the world has passed.

We do know that close observers have sensed a steadily progressing revolution of religion, a revolution which holds promise of getting back more squarely upon the basis on which rests the religion of Jesus, for there has come an awakening to the fact that in our attempted evaluation of Christianity, incidentals have been overemphasized and fundamentals shifted to places of secondary or tertiary importance. The original appeal made by Jesus for individual righteousness was for an end.

However much we may emphasize the need for personal righteousness, however deeply we may recognize that a prime purpose of the Christian religion is the formation of character on the pattern given us in the life of Christ and in his precepts, a proper envisagement of the religion of Jesus and the evaluation of his life force us to the conclusion that not even the most refined and most highly developed religious character can live the Christian religion by himself. "No man liveth to himself alone." It takes at least two men, and God to demonstrate the Christian religion, each man neighbor to the other, demonstrating his love of God in service to his brother.

Let us hope—aye, pray and work—that this conception of the Christian religion is expanding and shall expand in constantly widening circles until it shall seize the masses of the people of all nations; for then and then only shall war cease, when all shall recognize the deep meaning of those words of Scripture, "And hath made of *one blood* all nations of men," and made man that haply he might successfully feel after God; for when man begins to feel after God, the Spirit of God working in him will open his eyes to the fact that his fellowmen are his brothers and the love of God will issue in serving those brothers.

Social reforms have been proposed, but how seldom have these reforms escaped the taint of selfishness. The appeal has usually been made in the vernacular of selfishness. How could we expect otherwise? "Except a man be born again he cannot see the kingdom of God." It is necessary for us to know God, and to know him we must become aware of our brother and his needs. God and our brother are complements. To know God we must see our brother and to see God we must know our brother, a divine paradox.

Except there comes that divine personal renaissance which issues in a social consciousness, the new order of society cannot even be glimpsed. While we today look with delight upon that revolution in religion which distinctly tends toward a social interpretation of the Christian ethic, we cannot blink the fact that as yet there are far too few with a pure social consciousness. The majority still think, speak, and act in terms of self-serving interests. The awakening of this social consciousness has tremendous powers of soul expansion.

Paul once found his soul expanding to all the universe. May not his ecstatic expansion of soul have arisen from a deep spiritual impress of the social content of the message of Jesus?

We do know from our experiences that the content,

once grasped, lifts one up and out of oneself till the expanded soul readjusts itself in a new birth, a vision of larger things and an activity directed toward social betterment and weal, toward the achievement of a redeemed society, one in which the will of God has perfect play—his kingdom come.

● ● ●

There is perhaps no prayer so universal in its use as the pattern prayer which our Lord taught his disciples. Jesus meant it to be a model prayer, or one which would enshrine the true principles of worship, a prayer that would be in harmony with the will of God. When it is prayed with real intent, and supported by a life of devotion and faith, it is always a source of strength and it is faith-building and faith-renewing.

In some versions of the New Testament this prayer is couched in sixty-six words, the number of books in the Bible. It is extremely doubtful if a more condensed version of the prayer could ever be conceived, and it is equally doubtful if sixty-six words could ever enshrine such universal principles in such a brief utterance.

Did the Lord's Prayer spring spontaneously from the lips of the Master, or did he give it to his disciples after he had thoughtfully condensed it to an irreducible minimum of words? We do not know. But if one thinks it can be further reduced, let him try to reduce it to fewer words, and he will emerge from his effort with a finer appreciation of its beauty and scope. There is no doubt that this prayer was a revelation of the Divine.

While this prayer is quoted more than any other throughout Christendom, it is doubtful that its social import is fully recognized either by those who say it or by those who hear it said. It has been set to music many times, and some of these settings are truly beautiful. But one may dwell on its beauty and brevity, marvel at its compactness, and yet miss the social implications; and it is in these that the full significance of the prayer is seen. There is no portion of the prayer that is individual or strictly personal. Even the very first words make one conscious of his neighbor.

The version given in Matthew is slightly different from that recorded in Luke. Matthew records that Jesus went into a mountain and his disciples came to him for instruction. Jesus utters the Beatitudes and follows with other characteristic and beautiful sayings. He informs his disciples that they are to avoid outward show in prayer and in almsgiving and then says, "After this manner, therefore, pray ye."

Luke writes: "And it came to pass that as he was praying in a certain place, when he ceased, one of his disciples said unto him, Lord teach us to pray as John also taught his disciples. And he said unto them, When ye pray, *say.*" In the Matthew version the Lord is represented as including instructions concerning how to pray along with other admonitions, while Luke tells us that one of the disciples had asked the Master to teach them how to pray. Luke says that the disciples are told to say certain words, while Matthew writes that they are told, *after this manner* "pray ye."

Matthew's version would indicate that Jesus meant his prayer to be a model after which the disciples were to shape their own petitions. It seems that Jesus designedly formed the words of this prayer for his disciples as one which would embody the essential elements they (and we) should incorporate in our prayers to God; the various things for which we are to pray are, I believe, rightfully proportioned in the example he gave. Further, the order of emphasis is truly emphasized.

Dr. Frederick M. Smith has written:

It is a matter of considerable satisfaction to those who believe that the Christian gospel is social in its application to know that the first word of the Lord's Prayer socializes it. He did not tell us to use the first person singular pronoun, but he said "Our." We cannot utter that word understandingly without thinking of others. How many we might think of depends upon our situation, the general and specific conditions prevailing, or the training and experience and resultant attitude of the petitioner; or upon all these. It *must* mean at least *two.* So it may mean me and my wife; or it may mean, "me and my wife, my son John and his wife, us four and no more," as one man was wont to pray. Or it may mean those of a group large or small, the neighborhood, the whole nation, or the whole world. It depends upon the social growth of the individual praying. But this much it does mean, one cannot use the Lord's Prayer exactly, or use it as a model without having *someone* else in mind besides himself. He must in his praying be one of two or more.

And this idea or thought carries over into the next word, "Father." We are children of this Father of all, hence all others are our brothers. Here again there is play for breadth of vision, for the *ultimate scope* of what should be included in the children of the All-Father will be *all mankind.* Of one blood hath God created all nations. But far too many

194

do not believe that, and so to them *our* means less than all. Such petitions doubtless specifically limit the scope of the pronoun, though they may be more generous than the one cited.

In heaven fixes the one to whom we direct our petitions as the Supreme Being. Heaven we all think about as the abode of Deity, the center from which the whole universe is regulated.

Hallowed be thy name directs our attention to the necessity of all worshipers in prayer to utter words of adoration and love. The love for God in the heart of the true and understanding worshiper should be the very ecstasy of that refined passion. We owe tribute of praise and respect to the heavenly Father.

Thy kingdom come. These three words expressed the great objective of Christianity in the ultimate, though in the minds of far too many who call themselves Christian today the comprehension of the word "kingdom" is much too narrow and limited. There are some who in their belief that this refers only to a spiritual kingdom will still further limit it till it means not a group, large or small, who are banded and bonded by a common religious belief, but only a strange experience of the heart or an emotion defined in the parlance of the vulgar "getting religion"—a purely personal proposition or matter.

But Jesus meant far more than this. In his mind, as he taught his disciples to pray for the coming of the kingdom, *God's kingdom*, he envisaged the ultimate consummation of the great and universal plan Deity had for man's development and happiness from the beginning of time and creation. *Spiritual* that kingdom *must be*; but spirituality in man cannot exist as a separate and distinct qualification or attribute. It is inextricably mixed with factors physical, mental, personal, and social which influence in a thousand ways the quality of our spiritual life. The kingdom for whose coming we are to pray is a condition of mankind which will influence and determine every phase of man's existence and experience. To have only a motion of the heart or soul of a *person* in the midst of social evils, errors, and maladjustments is too much like a beautiful flower immersed and lost in muck. We Latter Day Saints, especially the Reorganized Latter Day Saints, have looked and still do look for the coming of the kingdom in the way of perfect social conditions, brought about by that gospel of Jesus Christ reforming men, individually and collectively, so that every conscious act will be motivated by good will toward men. So to us the "kingdom" is a reformed and perfect social order, based on active faith in God as the Ruler of the universe, Creator of man. It is what we call Zion.

When you pray, keep before you the prayer Jesus taught us. Repeat it, if you must, but better still use it as a model, and submerging your own self in the interest of others, pray for better conditions to come to us all; and with the effort you make to include others in that for which you pray will come an expansion of soul, refining and uplifting in influence, and distinctly Christian in quality.

● ● ●

We continue our discussion of the Lord's Prayer with thoughts presented by Dr. Frederick M. Smith. His writing shows deep and penetrating social insight and we commend it to you. He writes:

Following the three significant words of the Lord's Prayer, "Thy Kingdom Come," are those which give us the genius of the kingdom: "Thy will be done in earth as it is in heaven."

We are accustomed to think of heaven as a place where perfection reigns, where everything is done according to the will of God. To think of the abode of the great Creator of the universe as being anything else than in a state of perfection is incongruous: but we take it as a matter of fact, and fail to grasp the idea that the ultimate purpose of the great plan is to have that same will done on earth always, and unfailingly. This on man's part; but it can be brought about, and will be, by the gospel of Jesus Christ having perfect play in the lives of all of us. What finer condition of society can be conceived than that the will of God shall be continuously done on earth. It means the elimination of sin and evil, for they are contrary to the will of the Father. It means that perfection of man. The means of bringing such about is the operation among men of the principles of the gospel of Jesus Christ.

"Give us this day our daily bread." God has ordained that man in his physical being has need of certain things which will keep him physically alive. Man is a chemical and physical being as well as a spiritual one. The chemical changes going on within our bodies determine whether we experience happiness or misery. If all the functions of the body are perfect and well balanced, we live in comfort, not aware of organ functioning. We just "feel good." Food is that which furnishes the basis for natural chemical functioning within our physical beings. So food is a prime need, next to the oxygen of the air. For our needs we are taught to pray; and so we pray for our *daily bread*, physical food. But note, in the Lord's Prayer the form of the petition is for *our* daily sustenance. That person who in his devotional address to Deity prays only for *his* daily food is un-Christian, and so purely selfish that he cannot know Deity.

If and when we can utter the Lord's Prayer in the real spirit in which it was given, and with due appreciation of its genius, and ask for *our* daily bread, it is virtually to say: "Let me eat, but let it be only when my brothers also have that with which to assuage hunger and supply bodily needs. Let me go hungry when others hunger. And if there be too little for all, let me have only my share."

Are you at heart such a Christian? Are you willing also to say, "Give us shelter and clothing; but withhold from me when not all have, or there are those who lack? I would be comfortably fed, pleasingly warm, and securely sheltered; but the feeling of nutritional fullness would be made distressing by the knowledge of others' hunger; the pleasure of warmth would be chilled by learning that others are illy clad; the sense of security in adequate shelter would be shattered in the thought that others had not where to lay their heads."

I am glad that the Lord's Prayer would have us eat our daily bread while concerned about the welfare of others, as well as in the sweat of our faces.

"Forgive us our debts, as we forgive our debtors." In his weakness, man errs. It is human. Error must be rectified; forgiveness, therefore, is necessary. But much of our error (or sin) is committed against neighbor or brother. So we must pray for forgiveness; but the Lord has taught us to say: "I have need of forgiveness, O Lord; but forgive me not if I hold aught against my brother because of offense he has given me." The genius and spirit of the Lord's Prayer demands that only to the extent that we forgive are we to expect forgiveness on the part of Deity. Again the strong social content of the prayer is to the fore.

"Lead us not into temptation, but deliver us from evil." Sin came into the world through temptation. Constantly forces are in operation to deflect men from the attitude and conduct demanded by the standards of Christianity. Man must fight his way up. Two men, each yielding the other moral support, can better resist evil than can one. A united group is still stronger against the social evils about them.

But God does not lead us into temptation. We do not so believe, anyway. So we Latter Day Saints prefer the translation of the Scripture which has the prayer say, "Suffer us not to be led into temptation." But, remember, for *all* do we pray deliverance from evil, whether it comes through temptation or otherwise.

Today evil is about us everywhere. As long as human frailties permit envy, jealousy, strife, and ill-will to be in our midst, so long will there be evil to avoid. Therefore, we would avoid evil, even its very appearance. But again remember that the Lord has instructed us to pray that our neighbors, our brothers, all, shall not be led into temptation, and to be protected against the evils we fear. How magnificently social is the whole of the Lord's Prayer!

Any prayer would be incomplete without acknowledgment of our own humble relations to the Father. Appropriating none of the honor or glory of our existence, wisdom, excellence, or attainments, we attribute the kingdom, with his power and glory, to God, where it belongs.